LITERALLY

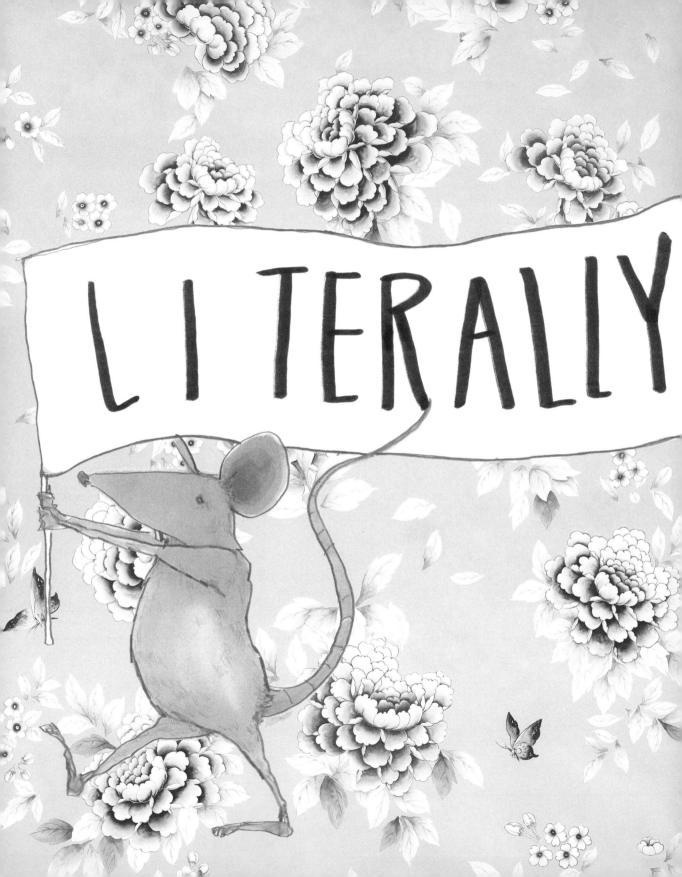

ME
JULIE HOUTS
TOUCHSTONE
NEW YORK LONDON
TORONTO SYDNEY
NEW DELHI

Touchstone
An Imprint of Simon & Schuster, Inc.
1230 Avenue of the Americas
New York, NY 10020

First Touchstone hardcover edition October 2017

TOUCHSTONE and colophon are registered trademarks of Simon & Schuster, Inc.

For information about special discounts for bulk purchases,
please contact Simon & Schuster Special Sales at 1-866-506-1949
or business@simonandschuster.com.

The Simon & Schuster Speakers Bureau can bring authors to your live event.
For more information or to book an event, contact the Simon & Schuster Speakers Bureau
at 866-248-3049 or visit our website at www.simonspeakers.com.

Endpapers design courtesy of de Gournay

Manufactured in the United States of America

1   3   5   7   9   10   8   6   4   2

Library of Congress Control Number: 2017942588

ISBN 978-1-5011-6951-9
ISBN 978-1-5011-6953-3 (ebook)

FOR

AMELIA
&
ELEANOR

LITERALLY ME

hi?

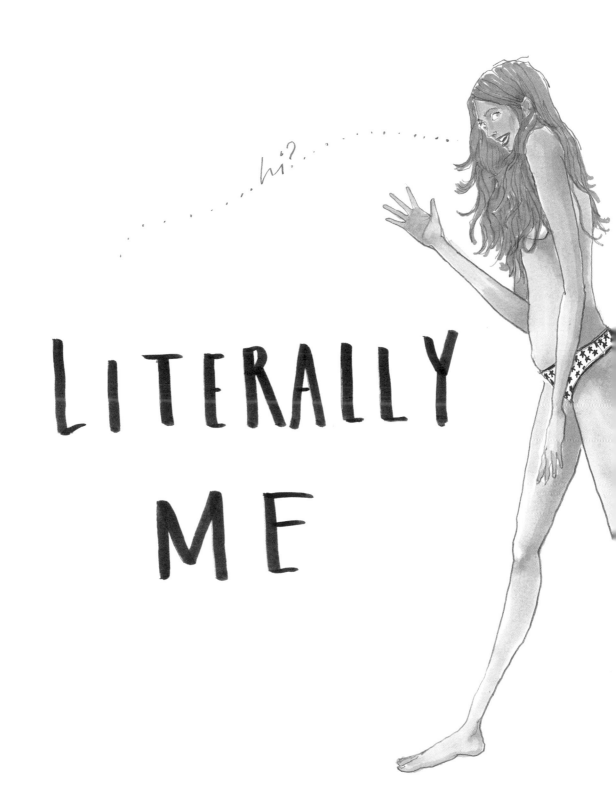

EVERYTHING HAPP

I HONESTLY JUST BEL

S FOR A REASON!!!
E THAT!

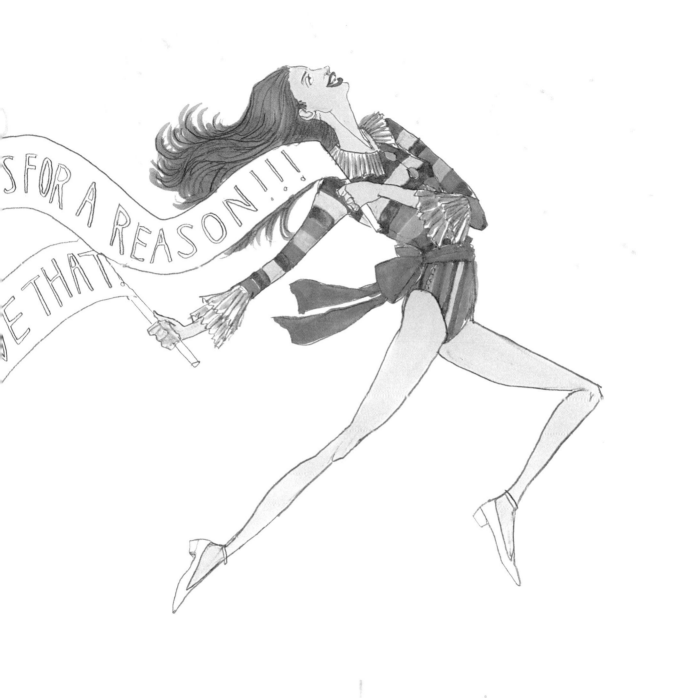

WHY......

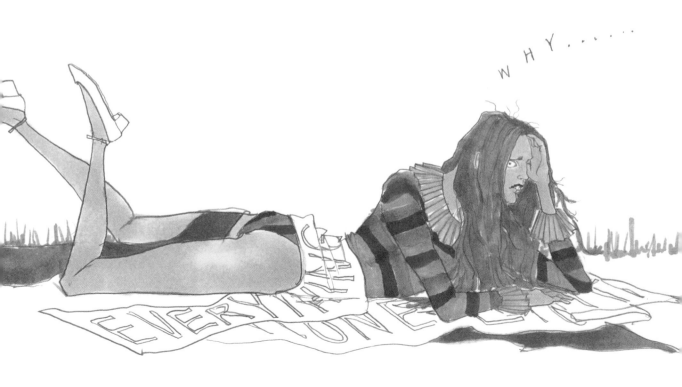

My Wedding Story

When Jared first proposed, I was shocked. Not necessarily about the proposal, but more because I immediately understood how much work I had to do before the wedding. Not even for the wedding. More like on ME. I was nowhere close to the person I wanted to look like when I married Jared. When I imagined myself as a bride, I imagined that moment when everyone would first see me, and I just felt like I wanted to hear audible gasps. Not necessarily because of how truly stunning I looked. I mean, that. Obviously that. But more like, about my transformation. Like, they all thought they knew what I looked like, and my basic body type, and then it's very "JOKE'S ON YOU! And you, too, Jared, because I am physically an entirely different person!"

So the first, and really most important, part of my transformation was my weight loss. I knew this would be the key to achieving that "Wait, I thought Jared was marrying Hayley. *Our* Hayley. And so who is this person? What is going on here?" reaction. As is, I am a fit person who takes care of her body. Jared jokes that it's obsessive and unhealthy, but then I typically make a joke about the fact that he routinely works eighty-plus-hour weeks with near-constant travel for his finance job and so we all have our funny quirks, and that's why we love each other. It's what makes us *us*. Then he usually says something like, "Someone has to pay for all this!" while waving his hands in the air. At this point, I usually just disengage entirely, because first of all, he's being crazy, and second, it's important not to stress out too much while planning your Big Day. I read that on The Ring.

So I started a detox diet eight months before the wedding. The diet said to eliminate sugar, dairy, carbs, meat, nuts, alcohol, caffeine, nightshades, algae, glass, plastic, synthetic velvet, and soy. I don't eat any of that anyway, but I do drink matcha and eat exclusively mushrooms, so I was worried at first. But I just stuck to my diet of hot water with lemon and compacted lampshade dust and was hardly ever hungry for eight months. But let me tell you—I ate every last organic mushroom I could find the day after the wedding. Which actually was only four, but they were delicious.

So in addition to the diet, I started getting tri-weekly colonics three months out from my Big Day. I wanted to feel weightless, and all that water was really making me feel bloated and yucky. I would recommend doing a colonic an hour before walking down the aisle. I did, and my stomach was so flat it was basically concave.

In terms of fitness, I stuck to my daily eight-mile five a.m. run but added private Pilates classes and barre classes as well as a boxing instructor. Closer to the wedding, I upped my cardio to include an additional eight-mile daily run, and that really helped to get those extra pounds off.

For beauty, I figured I needed to focus the most on my skin, as obviously my goal was to wear no makeup at my wedding and look completely flawless in photos and in real life. You know, people throw around the word "flawless" a lot, and I get it. I mean, I too revere Beyoncé in a religious way. But when I say "flawless," I mean TRULY WITHOUT FLAWS. That takes a lot of work and determination to achieve.

That's where the shock therapy comes in. I began seeing Mara Lynley-Rose three months before the big day. She uses electroshock therapy on your face to simultaneously stimulate and paralyze it. It's amazing.

And here, I must mention my love, Jared. After fifteen years of dating, we were at a level where I felt completely comfortable with him. Like no ask would be too big. So when I was unable to drink my water and eat my dust biscuits in the weeks before the wedding, he was right there, emailing his

assistant Megan to come feed me. I think I knew in those moments how much Jared truly loved me. Megan must have, too, because she usually cried silently the entire time she was feeding me.

I stuck to my routine with my existing facialist, Francoise Bouton, who is truly a goddess. Closer to the wedding, we introduced swan blood to my routine, and I really noticed a difference. My skin felt tighter, almost taut. Ever since I turned thirty-one this year, my skin has gotten so saggy and dry. Francoise said it was in my head. And I said, "Ha! I wish that were true! I'm an old dried-up hag now. But oh, well, Jared's stuck with me! Unless we get a divorce. But I truly don't think we will. Honestly." Then Francoise was like, "Just lie still, Hayley, and let the swan blood do its work."

I had my eyebrows all ripped out and put back in more evenly spaced. I felt like they were patchy, and just knowing that some hair follicles were closer together than others really bothered me. There's something grotesque about it. Do you know Soup? Not the food, the brow specialist in Tribeca. Her name is Soup Li. She is an actual living genius. Anyway, she did them. My eyebrows. People tell me how expressive they are.

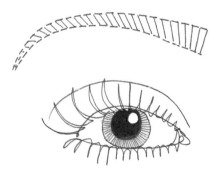

You know how they say that if your teeth are loose or falling out in your dreams, then you must be anxious? Well, I must be a REALLY anxious person, because two months before the wedding, my teeth literally began crumbling and

falling out of my mouth. It was disgusting. So I had to get all new teeth, which Jared was not thrilled about, to say the least. He kept saying my new teeth were costing almost as much as the wedding, which is completely insane, because the wedding I KNOW costs so much more, and beyond that, I was like, "Do you really want a bride with no teeth?" and he admitted that no, he did not. So the teeth were a thing.

I am a natural blonde, but for my wedding, I wanted to be blonder. Like, imagine when you stare at the sun and then look away, and then it's so light you can't see anything at all. That was my inspiration. So I met with five different colorists before meeting with Oscar Blanci, who gave me my blonde. We ended up just stripping my hair of all its natural blonde and then just painting on a sort of glaze made from the luminescent abdomen of a firefly that is indigenous to Bora Bora.

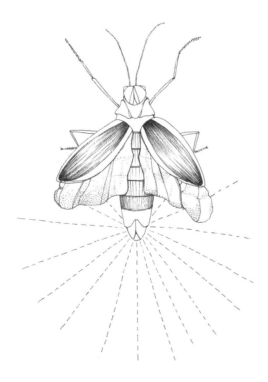

So when it was finally my Big Day, the biggest, most important day of my entire natural life, was I happy with my transformation? Mostly.

While perhaps I didn't lose those last 0.6 pounds, and my skin didn't glow as evenly on my face as it did on my left calf muscle, I'll forever cherish the look on Jared's face when he saw me coming down the aisle. I'll never forget how his jaw dropped and his eyes welled up with tears, and I'll never forget his first words to me when I met him at the altar: "What have you done?"

I knew in that moment that all the hard work was worth it, because he could see how much I had transformed, knew how hard I had worked to get to be the person who was standing in front of him that day. I've truly never felt so happy as I did in that moment—feeling so SEEN by Jared.

live
laugh
love
EXIST
SMIRK
LURK

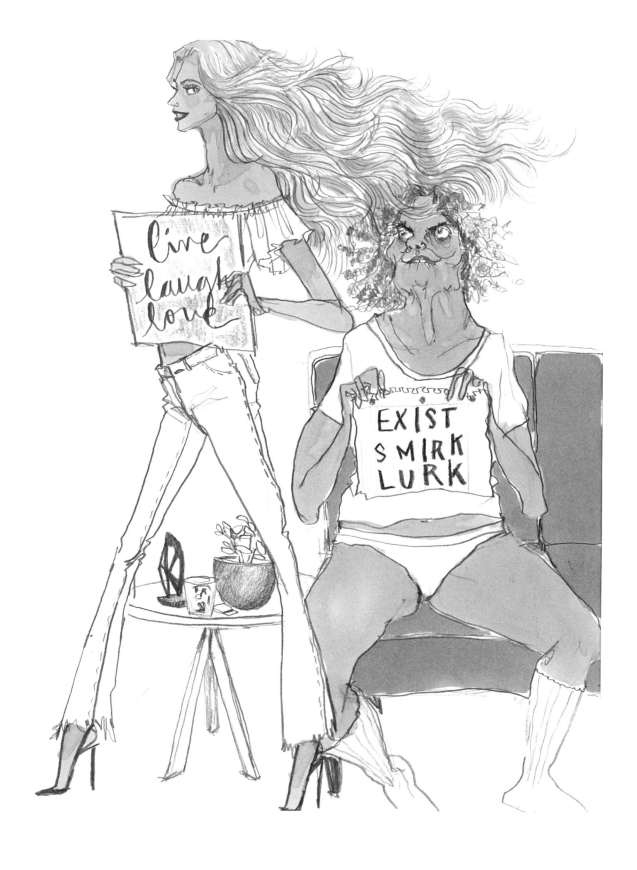

WHEN I MEET SOMEONE NEW & FINALLY COME OUT OF MY SHELL

WHAT COLOR ARE YOU GOING TO GET? I'M THINKING "TRICK HIM INTO MARRYING YOU (AND THEN TAKE HIS MONEY) BLUE" OR "DADDY'S GIRL." OH... WHAT IS "SKINNY DITZ"? THAT'S CUTE. IT'S LIKE "HELPLESS" BUT PALER.....
YEAH, I DON'T KNOW. EITHER "GET BACK IN THE KITCHEN PINK" OR "BUN IN THE OVEN." BUT LAST TIME I GOT "ILLITERATE SEX KITTEN" AND IT WAS SO CUTE. JUST LIKE, THE PERFECT NUDE.....

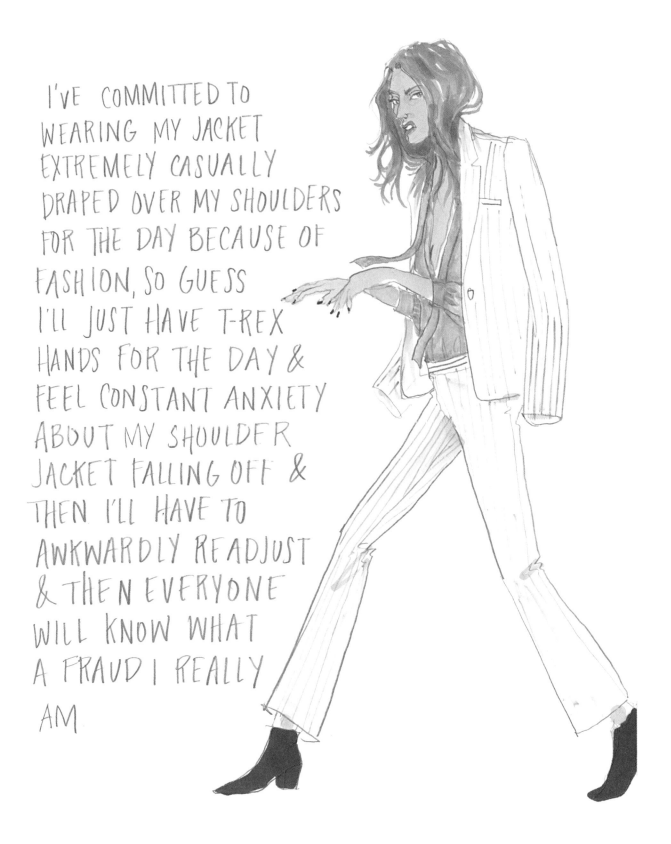

I'VE COMMITTED TO
WEARING MY JACKET
EXTREMELY CASUALLY
DRAPED OVER MY SHOULDERS
FOR THE DAY BECAUSE OF
FASHION, SO GUESS
I'LL JUST HAVE T-REX
HANDS FOR THE DAY &
FEEL CONSTANT ANXIETY
ABOUT MY SHOULDER
JACKET FALLING OFF &
THEN I'LL HAVE TO
AWKWARDLY READJUST
& THEN EVERYONE
WILL KNOW WHAT
A FRAUD I REALLY
AM

HOW MUCH LIPSTICK HAVE I EATEN IN MY LIFETIME?

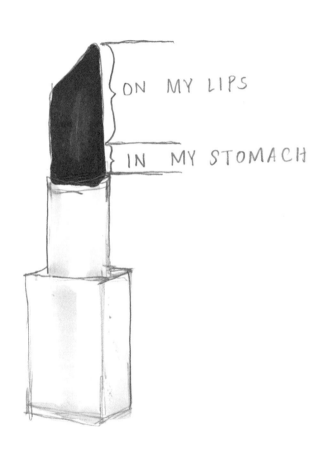

ON MY LIPS

IN MY STOMACH

I THINK ~~ONLY~~ ONE TUBE IN TOTAL

The Four Horsewomen of the Apocalypse

ANDI

I went every year. I've been going since I was eighteen. This year felt different somehow. I needed it. I was feeling so bogged down with school and work and all my friends were being so lame about it. They were like, "Ohhh, I don't really want to plan it," or "Ohhh, it's going to be so expensive . . ." Nobody would commit. For a second I considered just dropping it and not going this year. But there was just something inside me, like a voice, that was saying, "Go to the desert, bring forth my message to my people." Really weird! But I've been studying so much, I assumed it was just that I hadn't been getting enough sleep. I actually have been taking the tiniest amount of Xanax lately. Prescribed—not like, recreationally. But it really affects me.

I guess it was a weird idea to go by myself. I can't even eat lunch alone. I just felt like, whatever, and why not, and it will be an experience. All that.

So, since I waited until the last minute to book anything, and since all my friends bailed on me, I couldn't find a ride out. Everything was booked. Finally, I just called an Uber pool.

WHITNEY

We were all supposed to go. We had the entire trip booked. We had a helicopter booked, a house booked, a driver booked. It was supposed to be the best weekend. Then Kate ruined it by breaking up with her boyfriend, Jason, like four days before, and he was the one who had the helicopter hookup, and so obviously that fell through, and then he was like, "I'm actually going to take the house, too." I guess it was meant to be a "fuck you" to Kate, but I was like, "Okay, you're fucking this up for all of us, you realize??" And he was like, "Fuck you, too, Whitney. This is basically your fault. You're the one who seduced me in the first place." And I was like, "Seduce?? Nobody says 'seduce.' And also I was drunk, and you're being lame." He was just like, "Have a nice life, Whitney." And I was like, "Okay, you're being retarded." So, yeah, it all fell through, and then Kate didn't want to make a new plan with me involved because of what happened with Jason, so they're all going on their own as a big girl group. So I was just like, fuck it, I'm going anyway. I'm sure I'll run into people there that I know. I just felt like I had to be there. What? Was I supposed to just not go? It's Coachella.

It was too late to book a driver or anything, so I just called an Uber pool, which is disgusting but I was desperate.

RAYNA

I always go alone. I go to a lot of festivals, actually. Almost always alone. I used to go with my boyfriend, Rami, but we broke up. Or we stopped being together. "Break up" is not a term we use. We're not actively together. But we're always Together. Spiritually. Does that make sense? He's my whole heart.

Last year was my first year going without Rami. I loved it. I took mushrooms and just danced for three days. I accidentally got heatstroke and a really gnarly sunburn and ended up in the medic tent, covered in ice packs with an IV drip, but it was worth it. I felt like I had opened up a chamber of my heart that had been previously locked. Even to Rami.

I got an Uber pool the day of. It's cheap, and a good way to meet new people. I've met some really cool people in Uber pools. It just feels good to connect sometimes. Plus, I had a bunch of extra mushrooms and I figured I could probably sell some to somebody in the car.

GRACE

I'd never been to Coachella before. I've led what many believe is a very sheltered life. Maybe it has been in a lot of ways. I haven't had a lot of the experiences most girls my age have had. I didn't grow up with boys and proms and grades and football games.

I remember exactly where I was when Beyoncé first spoke to me. I was taking inventory of the bunker. My sister had been called away, and I was left to do the inventory alone. I grew up in a big family. Alone time is something to be treasured. It's also a breeding ground for Evil. I worried when I heard her speak for the first time. Was it Satan? I didn't know who the voice was. She called me by name: "Grace, join me."

It was just that for a while. Then one day while we were

getting gas in town, I heard the voice coming from the television. It was Beyoncé. I had never seen or heard something so beautiful. I had to be dragged away. I was punished severely.

The voice continued, and so did my disobedience. I was obsessed with her. Her name. Her voice. I made up excuses to leave the compound to go into town. I made up excuses once in town to try to find out more about Beyoncé. Asking strangers, borrowing their phones. This went on for years.

Beyoncé never spoke to me to encourage harm or evil toward myself or anyone else. She spoke only to encourage me, or to provide me with direction. I came to believe that God spoke to me through her. I couldn't share this with my family.

"Come to the desert."

My journey to Coachella started there. With that message. It took me five months to understand what it meant. I overheard two girls talking one day in the bathroom of a Burger King when we went into town for Benjamin's birthday lunch. They told me what Coachella was. They told me Beyoncé would be there.

Her voice got louder, more frequent. It took me five months to save up a bit of money from my job cleaning houses. I had to lie to my family. I saved enough to buy a cell phone from a gas station attendant named Ryan with whom I had forged a friendship in hopes of one day securing a cell phone. I sold my sister Esther to Ryan for an evening in exchange for $150, which afforded me a one-way plane ticket from Tampa to Los Angeles.

I intended to walk to Coachella from LAX if I couldn't hitchhike. I made friends with a girl on the airplane who took pity on me and called me an Uber pool.

ANDI

The Uber pool was fine. It didn't smell or anything, and the driver was cool. He didn't talk at all. I had my book with me, and I just planned on reading the whole way. I'm taking this comparative religion class right now and so I was reading the Bible. I really debated whether or not I should bring it with me in the car. I didn't want to look like some religious fanatic, just casually reading the Bible. But I had a paper due on the Book of Revelation, and there was no way I was going to finish it in time if I didn't get the reading done. I figured I could just sort of angle it downward or read it from my lap and hope nobody noticed.

WHITNEY

I got into the Uber pool and first thing I saw was Andi reading the fucking Bible. It literally said Holy Bible. I was just like, here we go. Obviously the first time I take an Uber pool I end up with a religious fanatic.

ANDI

I forgot to angle it downward.

WHITNEY

I just put in headphones and, like, hoped she wasn't going to try to convert me.

GRACE

When I got in the car, Whitney and Andi were already inside. I was nervous. I didn't think I had the right outfit on anymore. Neither smiled at me. I didn't know what to say to these girls. I thought a good opening question would be about who everyone was there to see. Maybe they were there for Beyoncé, too. Maybe they knew facts about her I didn't already know.

WHITNEY

Her look was like, um . . . if a homeschooled alien went to Walmart and bought a crop top? Bizarre. She was really skinny, though. Before her butt had even touched the seat, she asked if we were excited about seeing Beyoncé. She looked crazy. Super pale.

GRACE

Whitney ignored me. I didn't get a good feeling from her. I saw that Andi was reading the Bible but was trying to hide it. I know the feeling. I had always been told nobody in Los Angeles believes in God. That none of them were saved. I was happy to finally meet someone I could actually talk to. I think some small part of me hoped maybe Beyoncé spoke to her, too.

ANDI

Grace followed up her Beyoncé question by asking what my favorite Bible verse was, and, without waiting, began to recite hers. She seemed sweet, I just couldn't deal.

GRACE

And the stars of heaven fell unto the earth, even as a fig tree casteth her untimely figs, when she is shaken of a mighty wind.
—Revelation 6:13

Andi just ignored me, too. When Ryan sold me the phone, he surprised me by downloading *Lemonade* onto it. He stole me a pair of headphones. I know every word by heart. I've listened to it over four thousand times.

RAYNA

I got in the car last. The second I sat down I sensed really bad vibes. Like, REALLY bad vibes. But you know what? When I encounter energy like that, I try to remind myself that it's up to me what I want to do with that energy. In that moment, I chose to cleanse myself of the negative energy through a series of deep breaths. In through the nose, and out through a series of long AHHHHHHHHHHs.

WHITNEY

Between Rayna's chanting and Grace's crop top, I knew that what everyone was saying was true. Coachella truly is getting lamer every year.

ANDI

It was just quiet for a while. Sometimes Rayna would do her breathing thing. Grace was listening to "Love Drought" on repeat, through shitty gas station headphones. She was mouthing all the words. There were a lot of mouth noises.

GRACE

You, you, you, you and me could make it rain now
You, you, you, you, and me could stop this love drought.

RAYNA

I had made this really amazing mix of goji berries and toasted coconut and seeds. I call it my bird food. But honestly, a bag of that stuff, and I'm good for hours.

ANDI

Rayna had some seed bag like actual bird food. Was eating it. Mouth noises also. Whitney was drinking out of a venti Starbucks cup that was filled with rosé and melting ice. Did she think we thought it was tea?

WHITNEY

My girlfriends and I discovered this genius hack for sneaking rosé into almost anywhere. You just get a venti Starbucks cup. Save your morning coffee, rinse it out, whatever. If you fill it with ice and rosé, people just think it's iced tea. I always say it's guava, a new flavor. You could drink rosé at work if you wanted.

GRACE

You, you, you, you and me could make it rain now
You, you, you, you, and me could stop this love drought.

WHITNEY

After like an hour in the car, I was bored and like, tipsy-ish. The bottle of wine I had didn't all fit into the venti cup. Usually, I'm splitting it with one of the girls. Anyway, I drank half before I got in the car. There's not much to look at in the desert, and I couldn't talk to any of these freaks, so I started reading the Bible over Andi's shoulder.

And every creature which is in heaven, and on the earth, and under the earth, and such as are in the sea, and all that are in them, heard I saying, Blessing, and honour, and glory, and power, be unto him that sitteth upon the throne, and unto the Lamb for ever and ever.

And the four beasts said, Amen. And the four and twenty elders fell down and worshipped him that liveth for ever and ever.

—Revelation 5:13–14

WHITNEY

I was like, lol, what?

ANDI

Whitney at that point was visibly hammered, and started snort-laughing. I realized she was reading over my shoulder. So, I started to explain, and then was just like, actually, forget it.

WHITNEY

For some reason, I could not stop laughing about the word "sitteth." SITTETH!!! It is still funny. Are you kidding??? Sitteth?? It's so funny. Like, what if we still talked like that??

GRACE

I heard a commotion, and realized Whitney was snort-laughing and yelling "SITTETH LIVETH!"

RAYNA

It was hard to watch. Whitney is someone who is obviously hurting. I felt like I could see her pain through her laughter.

WHITNEY

Am I being crazy?? Is "sitteth" not a hilarious word?? The driver started getting pissed, which is retarded. Like, relax. We're literally in the middle of the desert. You're getting paid. It's fine.

ANDI

The driver was pissed. Understandably! Whitney was acting out of control. She had finished a venti cup of rosé. There's no way she weighs more than one hundred pounds. I was trying to just kind of laugh along to lighten the mood.

GRACE

I mean, "sitteth" *is* a funny word when you keep saying it over and over. . . . I laughed. It felt good. I relaxed a little.

RAYNA

It was such a powerful moment. Us four women, all beautiful in our own ways, all from different walks of life, thrown together by the Universe, uniting over an ancient word in an ancient text. I'm not a Christian, but I am spiritual. I believe in the Universe, and I just felt at this moment like there was a purpose for it all. That the Universe had brought us all together for a reason. We have to trust that the Universe will reveal its designs to us when It is ready. I decided to lead a chant that would help us in our journey together.

Om saha nav avatu saha nau bhunaktu saha viryam karavavahai
tejasvi navadhitam astu ma vidvishavahai.
Om shanti shanti shanti.

It means, and this is just my translation of the original Sanskrit:

May we together be protected,
May we together be nourished.
May we work together with vigor,
May our study be illuminating.
May we be free from discord,
Om, peace, peace, peace.

WHITNEY

Oh my GODDD! When Rayna started chanting, I LITERALLY DIED. I lost it. I couldn't stop laughing. She literally said *OM*!!! Swear to GOD she said *OM*. It was so funny. But I had drunk so much rosé, my bladder was so full. Then it started hurting from me laughing. I tried to stop . . .

ANDI

She fucking peed on me. This drunk bitch peed on me. I was sitting in her pee in the middle of the desert.

GRACE

I guess at that point Whitney peed on Andi? I mean, that is super gross . . . but it's also just a little pee. It happens. I'm from a family of sixteen children ranging in age from eight months to twenty-four years old, so in our house, yeah. Sometimes you get a little peed upon. Also, both our paternal and maternal grandparents live with us. Not in our house exactly, but in our compound. They pee on you sometimes, too, when you give them baths. It happens. Anyway, she didn't have to yell.

ANDI

She peed out an entire bottle of rosé. It was all over my legs, all over my bag, all over my fucking Bible, which, by the way, I STILL had not finished my reading assignment for because of Whitney and the sitteth thing.

RAYNA

Chants can be transformative. The heart opens, pulses. Like tidal waves, or torrential rains, chants wash the soul clean of negativity. Some people cry, some people pee. Our bodies release emotion in different ways. I thought it was beautiful that Whitney peed. I said a prayer of thanks to my Goddess and ate some of the mushrooms I had with me.

WHITNEY

I MEAN. Okay? "Sorry" or whatever? It literally has happened to
everyone at some point. Whatever. Andi was being so dramatic.
Like "Ohhhh, I peed on your Bible"? Grow up. Buy a new Bible.
They LITERALLY give them away on the street. The driver was
so ridiculous, too. I told him I would give him all my contact info
and would pay for the cleaning. What else was I supposed to do?
It happened. Move on. I don't regret the past. Or look back. I look
forward.

ANDI

So that's when the driver pulled over in the middle of the desert and
made us all get out so he could "inspect the damage," which, like?
It's pee. What do you think the damage is? Pee damage.

GRACE

I was trying to tell him ways to get it out of upholstery. If you
use vinegar and baking soda, it comes right up. We have a lot of
opossums in central Florida, and since we don't believe in doors in
my family, they tend to come into the house and get into the beds,
and sometimes there will be pee there. You know it's opossum pee
and not regular pee because it just has a distinct smell to it. Just
kinda more feral and musty than human pee. One time it got on my
face. I was taking a nap under a tree near the bunker, and I thought
it was raining but it turned out that an opossum was just sitting in

the tree above me peeing down onto my face. I remember thinking, God is teaching me something right now about my expectations and his plans. Sometimes you think you know what He's sending your way, but then you don't. And it's opossum pee instead.

I knew I needed to get to Coachella to see Beyoncé. I knew I had to leave the compound. I had to leave the family. I knew that once I was finally in front of her, God's plan would reveal itself to me. That through Beyoncé, God would speak to me. What I didn't know was that I'd have to walk through the desert first. Just like with the opossum pee. You have to be open to receive God's plan.

ANDI

Rayna was doing some sort of dance and chanting, Whitney was wandering around with her phone trying to find service, Grace was talking to the driver about opossums and God's plan and Beyoncé. Needless to say, he left us. I'm still covered in pee at this point, by the way.

WHITNEY

The driver literally got into the car and drove away. Do you understand how fucked up that is? He left us in the middle of the fucking desert. Nowhere near Coachella.

GRACE

Some people aren't ready to receive God's plans.

ANDI

At this point I got worried. None of us had cell reception. It was incredibly hot. I hadn't brought more than one water bottle with me. We just had to wait for cars to come by.

RAYNA

There are four seasons.
Four corners of the earth.
There are four Noble Truths.
Four foundations of Mindfulness.
Four matriarchs of Judaism.
There are four Vedas: Rigveda, Samaveda, Yajurveda, and
    Atharvaveda.

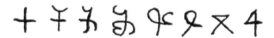

I was carving that into the sand.

ANDI

I realized Rayna was high when she began mumbling about the number four and writing symbols in the sand.

GRACE

It all made sense in that moment. Beyoncé's lucky number is four. She was born on September 4, and Jay Z was born on December 4. Blue Ivy's middle name is Ivy after the Roman numeral four. Both Beyoncé and Jay Z have the number tattooed on their hands.

There were four of us, four horsemen of the Apocalypse.

That's when the first horse came galloping toward us.

RAYNA

A beautiful beautiful beautiful pure white horse came galloping up from nowhere. It was the most graceful thing I have ever seen in my life. The horse stopped some distance away, right in front of a golden bow and crown. I felt like she understood me. She stared at me, through me. I didn't hear her speak, but I knew that I was hers and she was mine. I mounted her.

The last time I rode a horse was when I was living in Uruguay, years ago. But I knew I was safe.

WHITNEY

I was obviously like, what the fuck. The whole day had been like this—so fucking weird. I was basically sober at this point, and most of the pee had dried off me. But hello? A horse came from nowhere in the desert. That's not normal. Rayna walks right up to the horse, puts a fucking crown on her head, picks up a bow, and just mounts a horse. No saddle.

GRACE

I tried to calm down Whitney and Andi, explain that we were a part of God's plan, that the second horse would come soon.

WHITNEY

Grace tried to hold my hands, which was so fucking creepy. She had this creepy smile on her face like a serial killer. She was so calm, saying, "The second horse will come soon." I was like, bitch, we're in a desert and Rayna is wearing a crown and sitting on a magic horse. Like, how the fuck would you know if there's going to be a second horse or not?

But then there was a second horse. A red one. Like, the color red. Fire red. Louboutin red.

ANDI

I understood at that point. I think intellectually I grasped what was happening, but I can't explain it. I couldn't react. It didn't seem real. I checked my pee-soaked Bible.

And there went out another horse that was red: and power was given to him that sat thereon to take peace from the earth, and that they should kill one another: and there was given unto him a great sword.
—Revelation 6:4

When I looked over at Whitney, she was already walking toward the red horse.

WHITNEY

I don't know what happened. I just fell in love with Chrissy. That's what I call her. After Christian Louboutin and also Chrissy Teigen, because she has the same fiery color as the sole of the shoes but also the fiery badass no-apologies attitude of my queen Chrissy Teigen. I just related. I was like, Same, bitch.

I have literally never even touched a horse in my life because in all honesty, I have such a fear of all animals. I have a dog, but only because my friend Megan told me dog selfies get more likes than almost any other kind apart from naked selfies. I'm actually kind of scared of Coco even though she's just a little golden doodle. I make my mom take care of her.

I wasn't scared of Chrissy. I just knew what to do. The only thing I can think of that's similar is when I first started using Snapchat. It just felt intuitive in a way, like I had always had it.

I mounted Chrissy and literally did not look back. I was like, let's fucking go to Coachella, you creepy bitches.

ANDI

When I looked at Grace, I knew the next horse would be mine. Whatever the last horse was, that would be Grace's.

There was something creepy about Grace from the start. A sort of otherworldliness. Not just her outfit, which was just slightly off in every way. Her hair was too long, almost touching her butt, all one length. She was pale in a way that made me uncomfortable. Like she had been kept underground somewhere, away from the sun. She wasn't wearing any makeup except some Wet n Wild pink lipstick that she had kept pulling out and applying for five minutes at a time in the car, staring into space, that Beyoncé song on repeat. She had worn it almost down to a nub in the space of an hour and a half, and her mouth was ringed in frosted pink.

You, you, you, you and me could make it rain now
You, you, you, you, and me could stop this love drought.

When my black horse galloped up, I mounted her and held the golden balances in my hand.

GRACE

And I looked, and behold a pale horse and his name that sat on him was Death, and Hell followed with him. And power was given unto them over the fourth part of the earth, to kill with sword, and with hunger, and with death, and with the beasts of the earth.

—Revelation 6:8

I have known this verse since I was a kid. I've always liked it. Before we lived in Florida, when I was really young, maybe only six or seven, we lived in Texas in the badlands. We had horses then. We spent months building a pen out of found wood. Once, for only a few months, we had a pure white horse. We weren't allowed to name the horses, but we all did anyway. One of my sisters, Emily, named this horse Milky. At night, I'd watch Milky in the blue dark, and he didn't look white anymore, he looked pale. I wished he was the pale Death horse from Revelation. I knew he wasn't. He escaped one day.

Looking around the Coachella valley, I felt like I was right back in the the Texas badlands staring at Milky trotting up to me.

I don't know if I fully understood how God planned to use me past this point. But I put my faith in Him and Beyoncé.

We rode in silence toward Coachella.

ANDI

I don't know how long we were riding for. Five minutes?

WHITNEY

We were on the horses for probably six hours or so.

RAYNA

We traveled two days before finally seeing the carousel off in the distance among the palm trees. We had arrived. I ate more mushrooms.

WHITNEY

I mean, yes, it was definitely embarrassing showing up with these creepy girls on a horse. Obviously, yes, it was strange. I just hoped I didn't run into Kate and the girls. But I also sort of hoped I did, you know? My outfit was cute, and Chrissy is so much fucking cooler than a helicopter. Like, she is a red magic horse that found ME in the desert. You got there in a helicopter? Umm . . . cool.

ANDI

I didn't know what to expect. I didn't know what was happening. It felt like a dream. We rode straight into Coachella. Nobody stopped us. Nobody asked us questions. They just stared at us with looks on their faces like I have never seen before.

WHITNEY

We got there and everyone was obsessed. They just parted and let us ride through. It was so sick. I had cell service again, so I started a Snapchat story of me and Chrissy and the crowd. I felt like despite everything that had happened getting there, this was going to be the best Coachella ever.

RAYNA

Bad bad bad bad bad bad vibes at Coachella. Bad vibes. Really bad energy. I don't know if the mushrooms turned on me? I was trying to stay really positive and let my light shine. People were looking at me with these faces. They were horrible. Everyone's face was horrified. Their mouths were hanging open and it made them look like corpses. Bad bad bad vibes. Girls had paint on their faces. They looked like they were turning to dust.

GRACE

I looked down from my pale horse on the sunburned faces of the men and women below me with absolute calm. They looked up at me with a mix of horror and fear.

WHITNEY

My story was getting no views. At all. Not one. When I looked out on the crowd, nobody was looking at their phones. They were looking at us.

ANDI

Nobody noticed when Beyoncé stepped onstage.

GRACE

When I locked eyes with Beyoncé, I knew that Judgment Day had come.

ANDI

Nobody noticed when the sun went black, and the moon went blood red.

RAYNA

Narasimha Tava Dasohum
Narasimha Tava Dasohum
Narasimha Tava Dasohum
Narasimha Tava Dasohum.

ANDI

The earthquake began, but we didn't move. The crowd scrambled to find cover as stars fell to earth.

GRACE

And the stars of heaven fell unto the earth, even as a fig tree casteth her untimely figs, when she is shaken of a mighty wind.

—Revelation 6:13

HOW I START MY DAY:

- ~~TEN MINUTES OF MEDITATION~~
- ~~YOGA~~
- ~~COFFEE~~
- MENTALLY SUBMERGE INTO MY PHONE FOR TEN MINUTES UNTIL I FEEL LIKE I MIGHT HAVE AN ANXIETY ATTACK & THEN LAY BACK DOWN FOR FIVE MINUTES & LIST THE REASONS WHY I CAN'T JUST SLEEP FOREVER, THEN STAND UP.

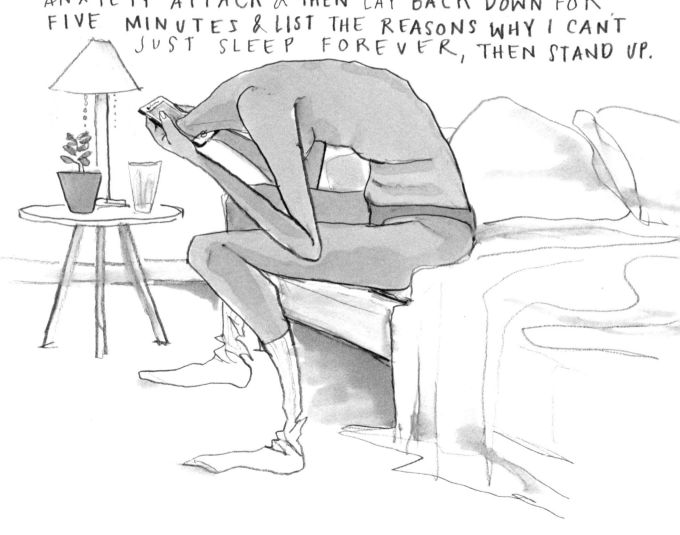

KYLIE JENNER
STEPS OUT EATING
COTTAGE CHEESE
RIGHT OUT OF THE
TUB USING HER
INDEX FINGER
& ALSO WEARING
FALL'S IT BAG

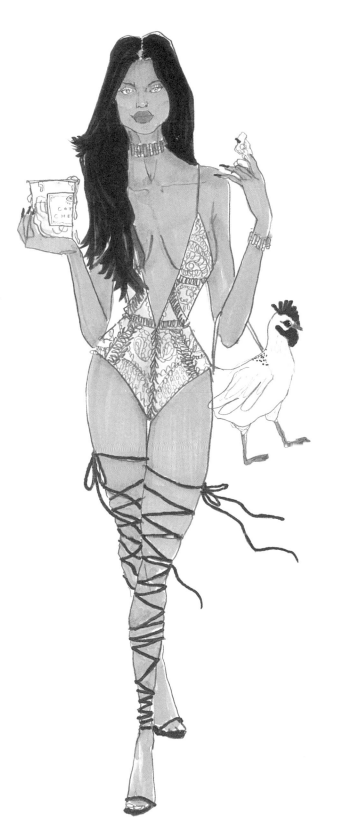

KYLIE JENNER
STEPS OUT WEARING
A PIECE OF DENTAL
FLOSS, A FEW PAPER
CLIPS & A PAIR OF
SOCKS, CHANNELS
PUNK AUDREY
HEPBURN

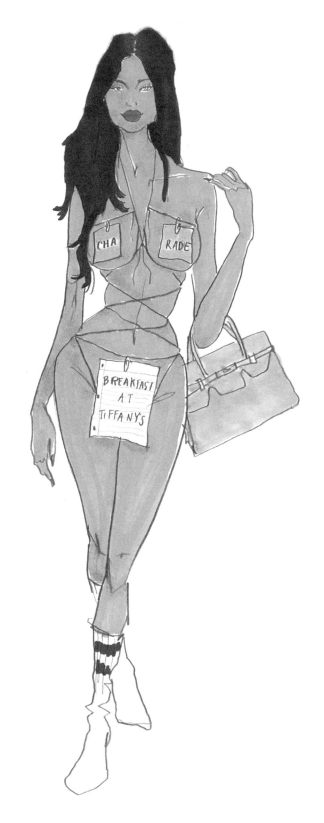

KYLIE JENNER
STEPS OUT WEARING
AN EYE PATCH, A BOLERO
& SOME JUICY COUTURE
SWEATPANTS, PROVING
THE EARLY AUGHTS
PIRATADOR TREND
IS HERE TO STAY

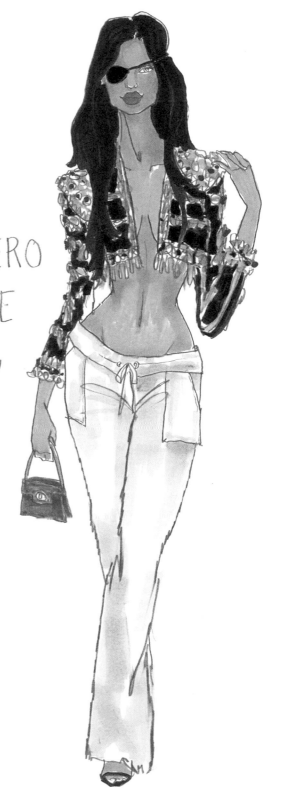

KYLIE JENNER
STEPS OUT WEARING
A SEVEN-PIECE
SUIT WITH AN
OPOSSUM ON A
LEASH, SHOWING
US ALL THAT
LESS ISN'T ALWAYS
MORE

①
②
③
④
⑤
⑥
⑦

KYLIE JENNER
STEPS OUT WEARING
A FOOTLONG SUBWAY
SANDWICH STRAPPED
TO HER HEAD &
SOME SERIOUSLY
KILLER THIGH-
HIGH BOOTS.

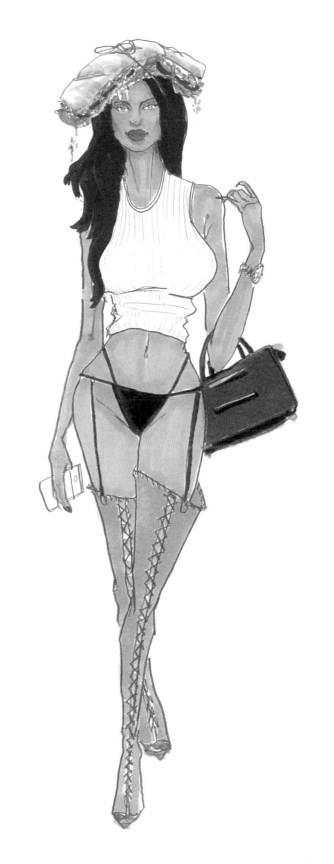

IS
KYLIE JENNER
DONE
STEPPING
OUT ?

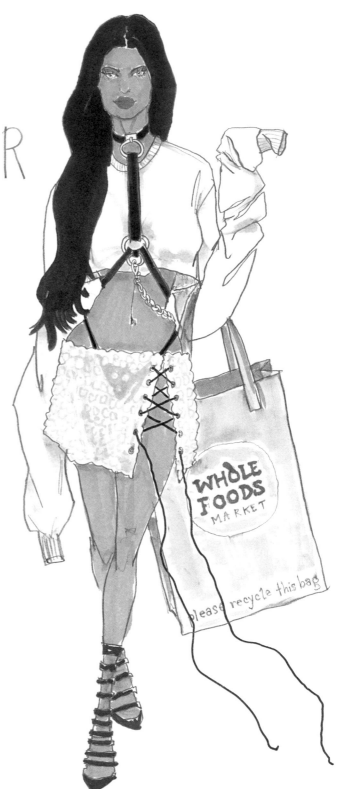

"I just got tired of stepping out," Jenner told X.com exclusively. She continued, "It was exhausting. After a while it just literally became about stepping out, and I forgot even how to step. So yeah, that was hard, the first time I realized I couldn't step. I just got really in my head about it. Like what does it even mean to step out? Like how? Which foot first? Like, do I have to bend my knee? What do my arms and hands do? How will I know when one leg is done and to bring the other leg to the front?

"My mom obviously called, like, a thousand doctors and they were all like, 'Oh, it's psychosnobatic,' and I was like, 'Um, okay, sweetie, then why can't I step out?' It was literally so dumb.

"Honestly? What's really helped has been the support of my fans during this time. I mean, a small part of me thought that maybe my followers would like, go down when I couldn't step out anymore. But everyone's been so cool with the like, marches and stuff they've been doing, like

#stepoutforkylie

#istepforkylie

"Like, that's so awesome. Someone told me the Step Out for Kylie March had more people than the Women's March, which is literally so crazy to me.

"Anyway, yeah, I guess every day is just another, like, well, actually like a step forward, and I guess I'm literally just trying to actually literally put one foot in front of the other and just get back to what I love, which is stepping out."

WATS UP
CAN I HANG?
NO
NOT SURE ITS RLY YOUR SCENE
YA NO OFFENSE
TEXT U LATER BABE

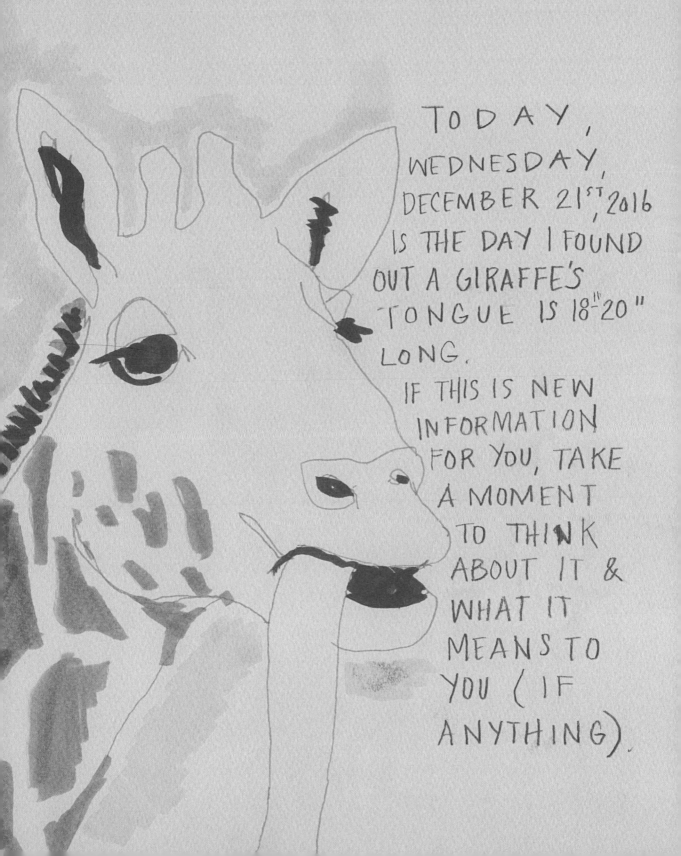

TODAY, WEDNESDAY, DECEMBER 21ST, 2016 IS THE DAY I FOUND OUT A GIRAFFE'S TONGUE IS 18"-20" LONG.

IF THIS IS NEW INFORMATION FOR YOU, TAKE A MOMENT TO THINK ABOUT IT & WHAT IT MEANS TO YOU (IF ANYTHING).

what ARE you doing?

I AM   BEING

SHY

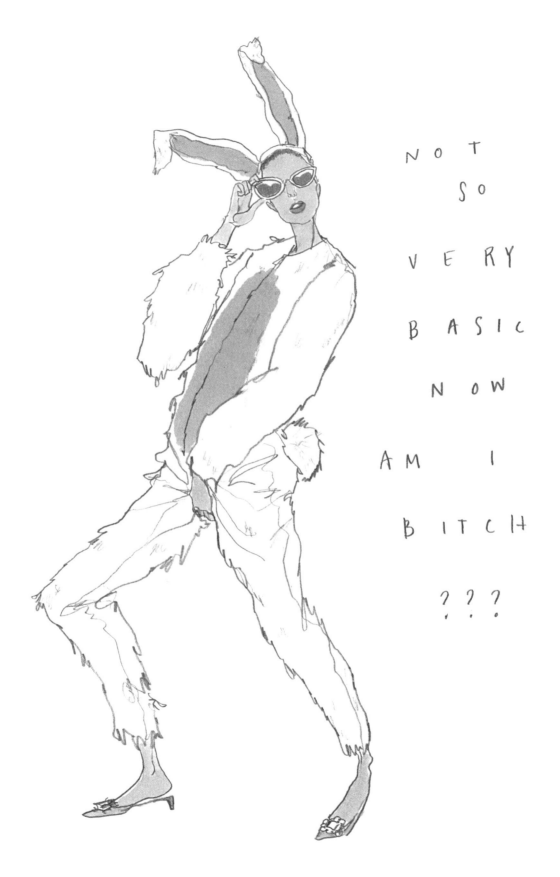

NOT
SO

VERY

BASIC

NOW

AM I

BITCH

???

A MEMORY:
FURIOUS, ENRAGED!
STEPPING ON EVERY CRACK I COULD FIND IN MY DRIVEWAY ALL AFTERNOON BECAUSE MY MOM WOULDN'T BUY ME GUSHERS AT THE STORE.
SHE CANNOT TREAT ME WITH SUCH INDECENCY.
THIS WILL TEACH HER A VALUABLE LESSON
MY WILLINGNESS TO BREAK MY OWN MOTHER'S BACK FOR A BOX OF GUSHERS
BACK-BREAKING ZONE

1.

this little piggy went to MKT
the newest ~~bar club~~ THING
in chinatown

2.

this little piggy stayed
home & watched five hours
of reality t.v., but when
asked, "what r u doing?"
she replied, "just reading."

3.

this little piggy had roast
beef for dinner, an order
she described as
"literally so random?"

4. This little piggy had none.
She actually only had haricots verts & water & therefore should not have to pay for THAT little piggy's roast beef. Though she prefaced this by assuring the group she was "not trying to be weird."

5. This little piggy took molly (or something - nobody saw) & then ran all the way home yelling, "WEE WEE WEE!"

6. This little piggy followed her friend all the way home, taking videos, uploading them to Snapchat & then privately texting their mutual friends "I'm honestly worried about her lately."

I'm adopted. I grew up knowing I was adopted, and therefore spent much of my childhood fantasizing about my birth mother.

My first fantasy birth mother was a neighborhood girl named Jenni, who was pretty and also my babysitter. My parents never really went out, so we only met probably about six times. She used to French-braid my hair.

Then I thought my aunt Cindie was my birth mother. Aunt Cindie was the youngest woman on my mom's side of the family, married to my Uncle Jim, who was funny.

They got married one year after I was born, and I thought perhaps Aunt Cindie did this in order to find a way back to me. The holidays were very important, because they were usually the only time I got to see Aunt Cindie, and I was always wandering around trying to find her so I could sit on her lap. She also used to French-braid my hair.

As soon as I was old enough to understand who and what Princess Diana was, I knew I had finally found my real actual true birth mother.

I wasn't that surprised when I realized who I was. Somehow I knew all along that I was the secret princess daughter of Princess Diana and [unknown (equally) glamorous birth father] who had been shipped off in the night to the suburbs of rural Indiana to live amongst cow pastures, golf courses, and Wendy's.

I never told anyone what I had discovered, and it wasn't necessarily something that was guiding me in my daily life. It was just a secret fact about myself, and when it was useful to call upon this knowledge and sit with it,

I would.

I used to think about Princess Diana on my birthday. I wondered if she was looking out the window of a stony castle somewhere in Scotland, like some modern-day Versace-wearing Rapunzel, thinking about her secret love child. What could she have done? She made an impossible decision in an impossible situation. I didn't fault her.

I was shy and blushed easily. I told myself I got this from her.

I used to worry that when I met my half-brothers we would have a hard time connecting because we came from such different backgrounds. Would they resent me? Would they be jealous that I didn't have a dumb-looking adulterous father, but instead an [unknown glamorous birth father]? We would all have to adjust. I would have to hold myself with a certain measure of poise that was not often asked of a Midwesterner. I'd have to figure out my forks, my curtsy. The only tea I'd ever had was Lipton's iced tea with several heaping tablespoons of Domino sugar resting at the bottom of the glass. There would be a lot to learn, but I was a fast learner.

I imagined that at some point, I would bring the boys to Wendy's. I'd explain how to dip fries into Frostys and how if you asked for it, "honey sauce" (was this stuff not just regular honey & why the extra "sauce" descriptor?) would be provided for chicken nuggets. I could take them biking through cornfields. Did they even ride bikes in England? These were details for my princess's secretary to sort out.

I practiced my British accent alone in my room sometimes. I considered myself to be preternaturally good at a British accent, and this was just further proof of my lineage. "You're so good at that!" my friends would exclaim. "I don't know, it's just natural to me..." I would say, with my Shy Di blush.

On the morning of Sunday, August 31, 1997, I was at Jessi McComb's house inside of a Beauty and the Beast sleeping bag, lying on the carpeted floor. Jessi was an only child who looked like both her parents. Her dad biked a lot and was often clicking around their house in his cycling cleats and a pair of mini spandex shorts, eating fruit, and that always made me feel weird.

Either he or the mom told us. I don't remember which.

I didn't cry at Jessi McComb's. I think on some level, I thought I would be giving myself away. Everyone would be able to tell through the intensity of my sobs that there was something more going on. Oh no, can it be that we are comforting the secret princess daughter of Princess Diana and [unknown glamorous birth father]?

I held myself together until I got home and took a bath. Then I cried. Then I stopped. Then I started thinking about something else. I never had another fantasy birth mother, and I gave up hope that day that I would ever meet my real birth mother. In my head, she had died that morning.

NAME_____   DATE_____

EVERYTHING HAPPENS FOR A REASON

Directions: For each statement in the "EVERYTHING" column, choose a statement from the "REASON" column which might answer the question, "WHY?" Draw a connecting line.

EVERYTHING

LATE TO WORK, GET YELLED AT

NUCLEAR HOLOCAUST

HATE WOMEN NOW, WORK OUT A LOT

LOOK LIKE AN IDIOT ALL DAY

FIND JESUS

BUY A MALTESE, NAME IT SPINACH

SPEND WEEKS IN SILENCE, PARALYZED BY GRIEF

BECOME A NEO-NAZI

REASON

WOKE UP 45 MINUTES LATE

DUMPED BY FIANCÉ

SPILLED COFFEE ON NEW WHITE SHIRT

ELECTED A HUMAN GARBAGE PILE AS PRESIDENT

FLIGHT DELAYED

ORDERED SALMON, BUT SERVED DUCK CONFIT

LOST A CHILD TO ILLNESS

MOM NEVER SAID "I LOVE YOU," NOT EVEN ONCE

WATER YOU DOING?

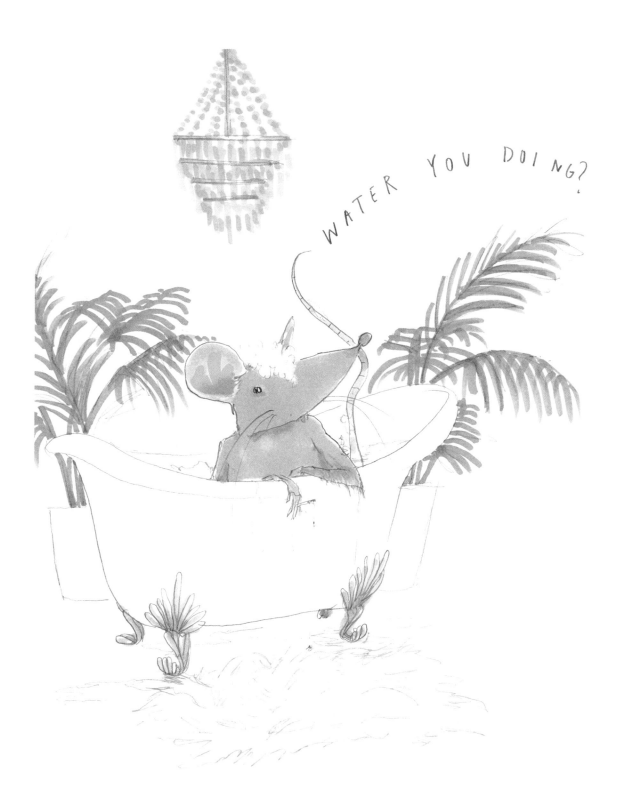

I AM TRYING
TO
GET
DRESSED

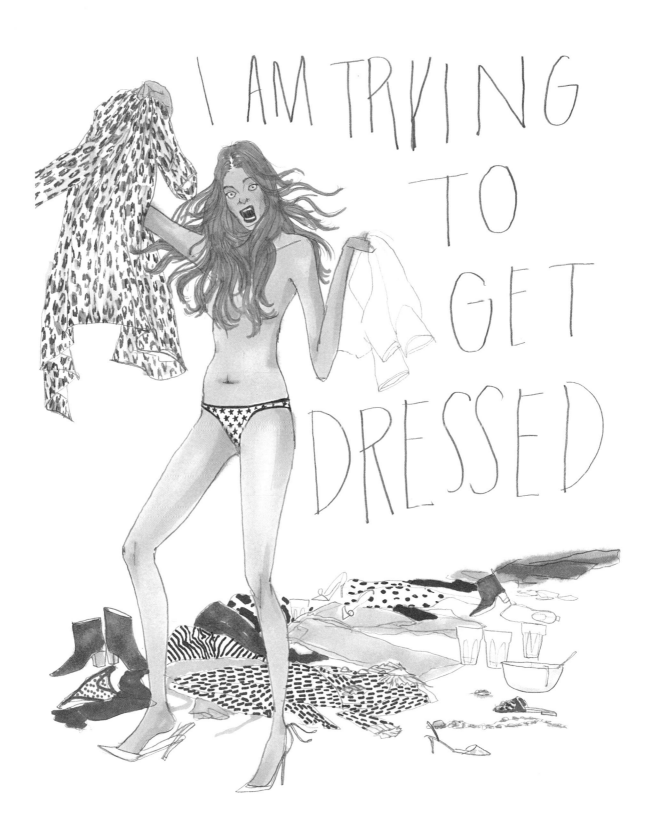

THE RULES TO THE GAME
THAT I HAVE WON:

① MAINTAIN EMOTIONAL DISTANCE
FROM ALMOST EVERYONE
FOR REASONS NOT EVEN
YOU UNDERSTAND

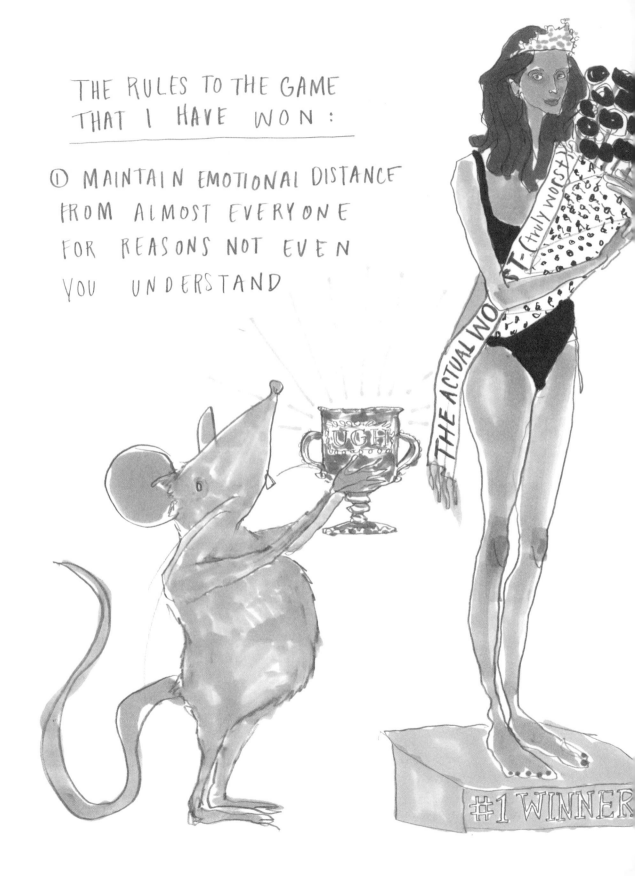

WOW - WHERE TO BEGIN?
I GUESS FIRST, I'D LIKE TO THANK MY
BRAIN. I TRULY DO NOT THINK I WOULD
HAVE EVER MADE IT THIS FAR WITHOUT
YOU. YOU ALWAYS PUSH ME. RIGHT WHEN
I THINK, "YOU KNOW WHAT? FUCK IT. OPEN
UP!" YOU'RE ALWAYS RIGHT THERE LIKE,
"WOW. NO. STOP. BACK UP." & SO THANK YOU
FOR THAT. I GUESS I SHOULD ALSO THANK
SEAMLESS & iMESSAGE FOR BEING THERE
FOR ME WHEN I JUST PANIC & BAIL
ON PLANS WITH SOMEONE I DON'T KNOW
VERY WELL YET. YOU GUYS HAVE BEEN
VERY COOL TO ME IN THAT REGARD.
BUT YEAH - MOSTLY JUST A HUGE
MURKY "THANK YOU" TO MY BRAIN AS
AN ORGAN. I DON'T UNDERSTAND YOU
BUT THANKS.   GOOD NIGHT
                      EVERYBODY!

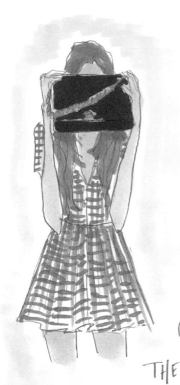

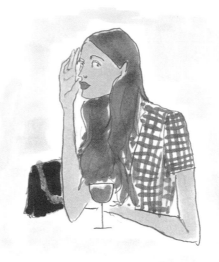

SCENES FROM WHEN I GO OUT & AVOID THE PERSON I'M INTO SO THEY KNOW I'M INTO THEM.

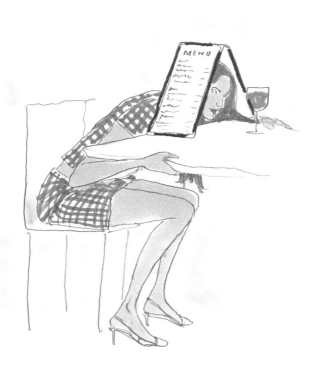

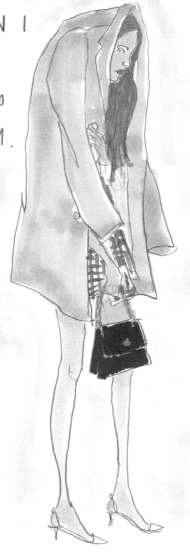

WHEN I KEEP IT
LOW-KEY ON A
FIRST DATE SO I DON'T
SCARE HIM AWAY WITH
FASHIONS

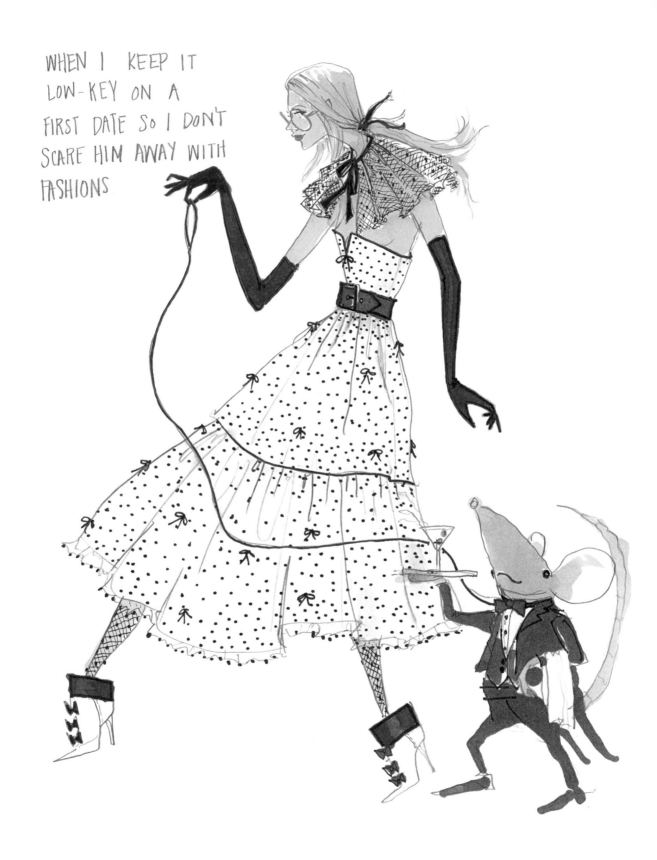

HOW TO GRACEFULLY EXCUSE YOURSELF FROM A BAD DATE
HOW INCREDIBLE. NO, I HAVE NEVER COOKED TROUT. OH YOU MAKE COLLAGES?
ex. A
OH NO OH GOD A NOSEBLEED WHAT COULD BE WORSE? I REALLY MUST GO
PRO TIP:
YOU MAY HAVE TO PUNCH MORE THAN ONCE; DO NOT BE DISCOURAGED!
ex. B

My stuff? I don't really have STUFF. I have complexities. I have issues that make me difficult, avoidant, brooding. But "STUFF"? NO. But like, here's something – I've got a lot of issues with my mother. But, you know, like any other dude in his mid-thirties I haven't taken the time to examine that, or, yeah, even really acknowledge that. So you know, I have a hatred of women. It's super subtle. You wouldn't notice it right away. & I mean, I identify myself as a feminist. I have a pin that I wear. It says "FEMINIST." Girls love it. But yeah, the hatred of women. Mine. It's a Thing. But that's not going to be weird, is it? Like in terms of whatever it is we're doing? "US" or whatever? Not that I would even

necessarily say we're
"together." I wouldn't.
Do you understand what I'm saying?
No, I think I get what you mean.
You're really complicated.
I love that. Let's begin
a relationship
at once.

COMFY?
NO, I HAVE TO POOP.

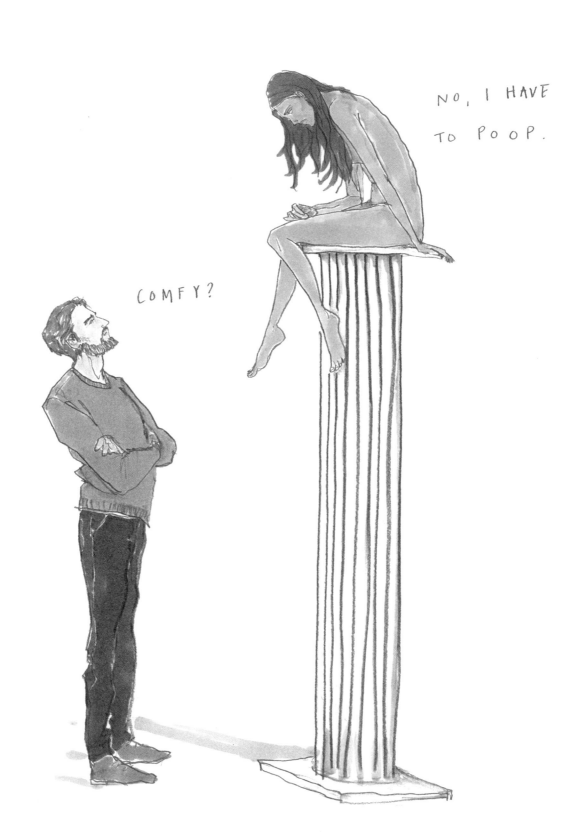

SOO...
YOU'RE AN
ARTIST?

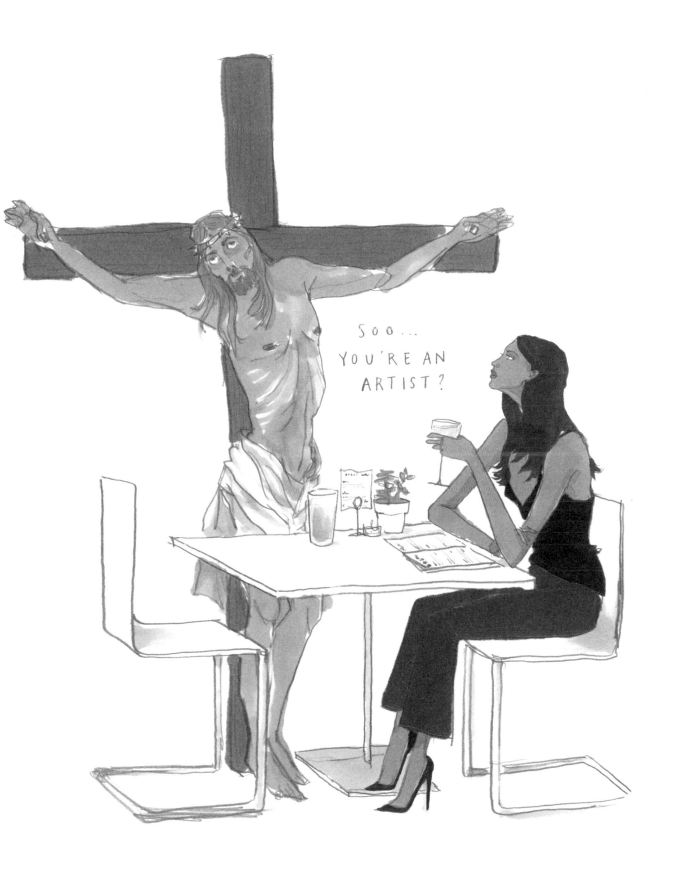

hey u up?

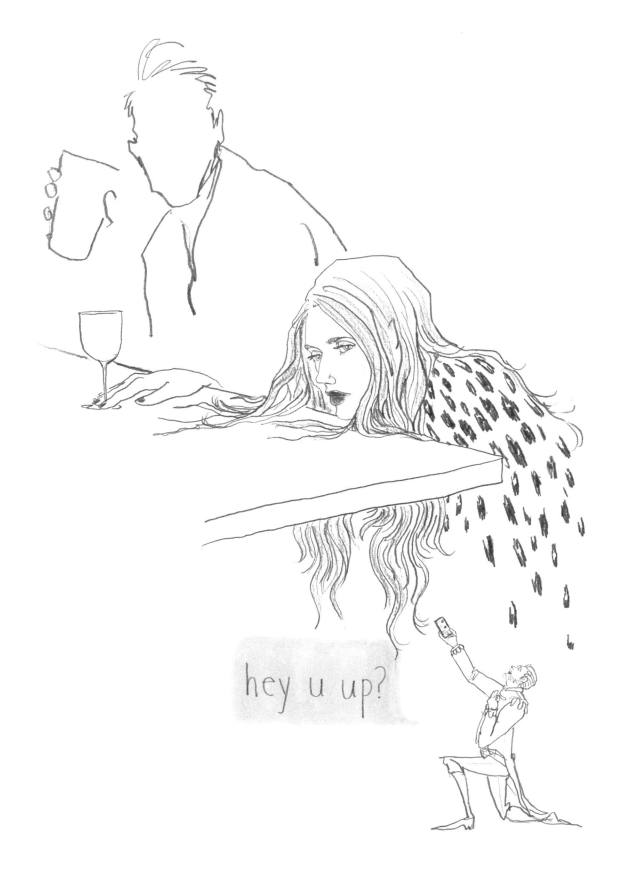

I NEVER SAID YOU DID
I DON'T LIVE INSIDE YOUR HEAD

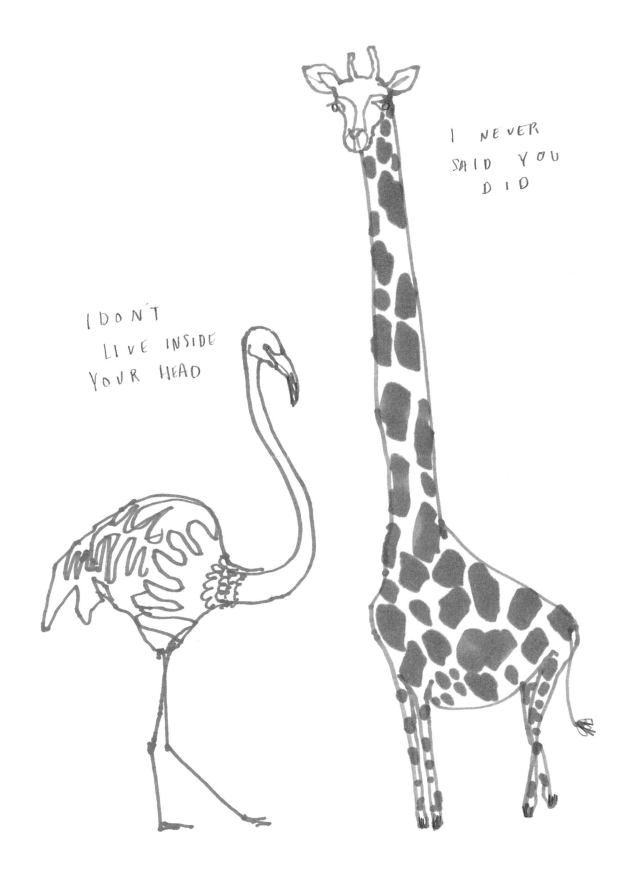

Assimilation Code

Let's begin with Basic Socialization.

When you enter a room, you find the ones that are yours.

You need to pay attention. Most often, they will be in groups of three or more. If they are in groups of three or more, you can join the groups provided that you know either the majority of the group, or one or two are Intimates of yours. If they are your Intimates, you can join the group because you have a right to be there.

If you see a cluster of three or more and you have no Intimates in the group, only acquaintances, don't join the cluster. Continue scanning until you find a cluster that meets the criteria of joining. If you can't find one, go to the bar and get a drink.

Notice: Do they have drinks that are like beers and wine? Do they have drinks that are like martinis and cocktails? If the former, follow suit and order a beer or a wine. It is important to notice the season or weather. Since you are Girl, you drink wine. Is it cold? You order a red wine. Is it hot? You can order a white wine or the pink wine called Rosé. The pink wine is considered to be the most fun kind of the wines. Later, in conversation, it might be remarked upon as if you have made a decision that says, "I'm embracing the season. I'm enjoying life." It is appropriate to make a remark in turn about the weather being the reason for your decision to drink the pink Rosé wine. So, as you can see, it's important to get this right. Drinking the pink wine in bad weather will elicit suspicion and further questioning.

If they are drinking cocktails, it means it is going to be a longer evening where they will all get more inebriated. The average amount one can have before It begins to lose cognition if It's a Girl is around three. Man can have more cocktails, but sometimes that isn't the case.

For us, we can drink a martini. It won't affect us, but don't have more than three because, again, it will elicit suspicion. It's important with each one to perform your Inebriation indicators with increasing frequency. Martinis send a message to them that you enjoy drinking and are present to have some fun. They usually like to see a martini. It makes them feel good about their lives. The message of it says, "We're all here because we can be to enjoy ourselves because we deserve it." They enjoy to feel this way.

Once you have selected your drink at the bar, you must determine which cluster to join. It is imperative that you do this swiftly, because it will be noticeable if you are alone for too long once you have completed your drink mission.

To enter a cluster, you must walk up and establish physical contact on the person with whom you are most Intimate. You address the whole cluster in the High Register of your voice to indicate excitement and general positivity. This generates Positive Reactions amongst them toward you.

Scan their faces to be sure there are no Negatives. You can spot a Negative a few ways. The first way is when you do your Facial Cognition scan on them, sometimes they will register as Blank. The read will look like "Disinterested" or "Bored" or "Judgmental." Those are just some options. There are others, but in general, if you do your scan and it comes back with primarily Negative Responses, you can then do a deeper scan and try to discern the reasoning and the proper course of action to garner a Positive Response.

Again, there are lots of ways, and the System will generally pull the three best Courses of Action, or COAs. Sometimes the System will pull from your Memory Drive the last interaction and prompt you to ask a Follow-Up Question in regards to a subject you spoke about with It the last time you saw It. Something like, "Oh, did you guys get that apartment?" or "How did that interview go, by the way?" Sometimes if the Memory Drive is coming up blank, it will just offer a default exclamation, which is typically something like "I haven't seen you in forever!" or an Admiration Exclamation, like "You look amazing!"

The System is good, and usually works extremely fast, but occasionally there will be glitches, or it will be in overdrive, doing Facial Cog on the rest of the cluster. If this is the case, it's important to maintain High Register Voice (HRV) and keep all your Excitement Facial Features (EFF) turned on until it finishes its scan and presents the overall data (OD) of the cluster. The only one I would say could be switched off is the Eyebrow Raise Function. Sometimes that can elicit questions if you leave it on too long. But Eye Sparkle and either Teeth Smile 1 or Closed Smile 2 should remain on until the System tells you otherwise.

Let's run some hypotheticals.

Hypothetical #1

If the System delivers the OD and it presents two potential Negatives in the cluster, and the cluster is comprised of four, the system will ask if you want to run cross-analytics on the two Negatives. You should always say yes. If you can determine if the two Negatives are Intimates (I find that they frequently are), you'll know that they have probably come to their Negative status together and compared their analyses of you, thereby increasing their Negativity.

This is a tricky situation, though it is relatively common in the beginning of your Assimilation. You need to run a full scan on each Negative within the context of all Group Members present at the function. Determine which Negative's stats are stronger in terms of general Likability and Influence within the group present. These are really the only two categories you need to worry about immediately.

Once you've determined which Negative is more valuable (N1), you need to narrow your conversation scope to the N1's interests (found in your Profiles bank in Memory). Try to steer the conversation toward Its interests and allow space in the conversation for It to be able to talk at length and Demonstrate Value to the other members of the cluster.

Use your Conversation Analytics to track the trajectory of the conversation and ensure that it stays within the confines of N1's Interest Brackets. I think you'll find that your Approval Rating with N1 will be increasing by the second. If you toggle over to the other identified Negative (N2), it is my experience that 90 percent of the time, your Approval Rating with N2 will be plummeting even further. At this point, you want to keep it right above Confrontation Level. Somewhere right around "Highly Annoyed."

Though this might seem dangerous, it is actually the correct COA in this specific Hypothetical. Here's why: by now you have garnered (hopefully) either a Neutral or Positive Approval Rating from N1. The cluster will sense N2's Highly Annoyed Level. At this point, run a fast scan on N2 and determine Its Triggers. Select a Trigger that is Medium to Medium Low in Intensity, and generate a question incorporating this Trigger. The question must be Friendly in its delivery. This is important.

Once you release the Friendly Trigger question to N2, 85 percent of the time the N2 will have a Hostile Reaction. You have to just override the System here. Trust me on that. Your Approval Rating with N2 will be at Confrontation Level, but that's exactly what you want. Once N2 unleashes Its Hostile Reaction, the rest of the cluster (all now Positive or Neutral-Positive toward you) will feel that N2's Reaction was inappropriate, and they will begin to run internal-cluster systems to isolate N2 and ensure that you feel Comfortable after N2's unwarranted Hostile Reaction toward you.

At this point, you can either engage Graceful Exit or stay within the cluster and wait for N2 to excuse Itself. I have run this simulation countless times both in Hypotheticals and at functions, and its success rate is 95 percent.

Impressive, isn't it? It's a good example of how to use the System as a tool, but also how to rely on your Experiential Data Bank. I have been accused in the past of relying too much on my Experiential Data Bank. I'm sure you've heard that about me. But I get results. I have been Assimilated for five years now with Approval Ratings in my Group in the top 5 percent, and as you'll see, I have secured a Long-Term Partner (LTP).

N1
N2
Engage Graceful Exit?
Close
OK

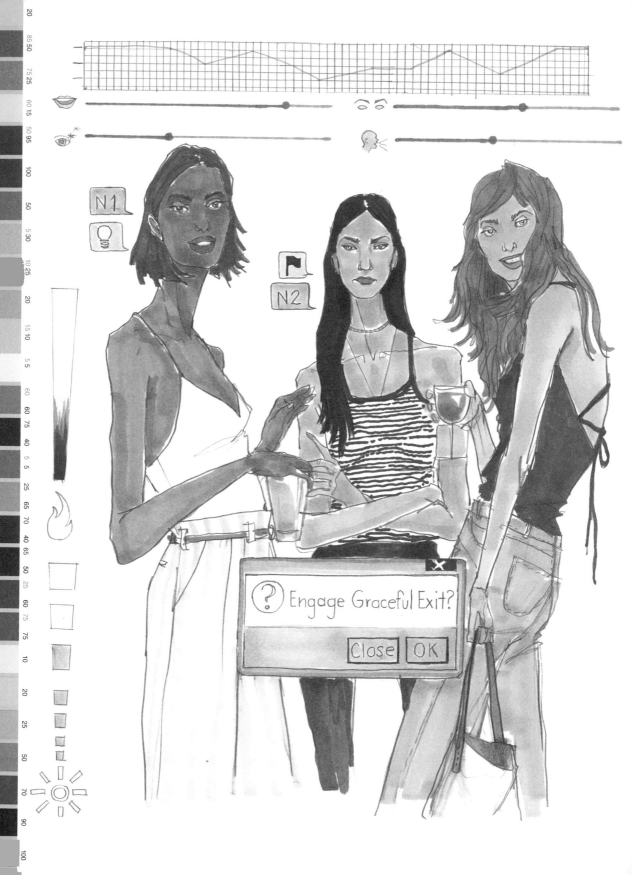

I met Brian two Human Years ago. The years prior to that, I had been gathering data by harvesting Short-Term Partners (STP). A lot of ##### hate this part of Assimilation. Admittedly, it was grueling. It's a lot of work to even secure Potentials, let alone Short-Term Partners, but if you do the work, it pays off.

I started running Simulations on my own time even before I began my Assimilation. How to track Potentials and monitor and feed their Interest Levels. ##### have been running the same Games that have been in our Programming since the beginning of time. While I'll admit those Games do often achieve results in Potentials, it is nearly impossible to secure even an STP running the same Gaming Programs over and over again on them. It's my personal belief that they're getting more Intelligent. When I started Dating, the Games I would run on Potentials would ensure me at least two Human Months with them to harvest data. Now I talk to some ##### who will try to run the original Games on Potentials, and they don't even get two Human Weeks.

That's why I decided to write my own Games. Without them, I would still be a Single and never would have met Brian, whom, as I said, I have been harvesting for a full two years.

The old Gaming Programs had us Displaying Interest immediately, then scaling back our Interest Level dramatically once we had Confirmed Interest from the Potential (P1) and adding an additional decoy Potential (P2) to the Game. This would create Desperation in P1 and engage Its Territorial Instincts, which was when we would Display Vulnerability, spiking P1's Interest Level to its peak. With P1's Peak Interest stats, we would unlock permission to engage in Coitus 1, which would end the Game, the Potential now secured as an STP.

When it worked, it worked. But there were all sorts of problems with those Gaming Programs. For example, if P2 wasn't chosen carefully enough, It had the potential to go Nuclear, informing other Potentials or Group Members about the Game, dramatically decreasing one's overall Likability Levels and decreasing general Goodwill toward the #####.

P1
P2
P3
X
Would you like to send this potential a message?
Close
Yes

What I learned is that most Potentials are primarily focused on themselves until Coitus 1. With this data, I decided to create two new Games.

Game 1: Potential-Centric Abstract Concept Cultivation, or PCACC

This Gaming System operates under the assumption that Potentials have singular focus on Themselves only, and therefore, the fastest way to unlock Coitus 1 and begin harvesting is to make yourself as Likable to the Potential as possible.

Upon meeting the Potential and confirming Its Attraction Level, you scale your own Interest Level very high. The System will prompt you, "Would you like to send this Potential a message?" Select "Yes." The System will have you select "Sexual Advancement" or "Deep Emotional Connection." This is how you unlock the Game. You select both simultaneously.

I know, every part of you says, "No, it's too much. Its Interest Level will plummet," "It might have a Fear Response." Trust me, the first time I did it, I was scared. But I trusted the data.

One hundred percent of the time, the Potential's Attraction and Interest Levels will spike dramatically. This is truly where the Game begins.

It is important at this point to disorient the Potential. Its General Cognition levels will be low, as all of Its Resources will be feeding Its Attraction and Interest Levels. It will be agreeable to engaging further in the Game. You should remove the Potential from the current environment and relocate. Once removed from Its familiar surroundings, the Potential will begin to perceive you and the Game as an Abstract Concept (AC). If a Potential can view you as an Abstract Concept, it means It is disinterested in running any hard analytics on you, and you will later be able to harvest with almost no resistance.

I cannot overstate the importance of securing AC Perception in the Potential. The Potential's desire to project Its own Hopes and Desires upon you allows you to free up more space in your Memory Bank and also allows you to be running other Programs while still harvesting your Potential, as It will view you however It wants regardless of your General Output.

After securing AC Perception, you must be constantly running scans on your Potential and following up with Thoughtful Questions and Admiration Exclamations. This is important. Your Physical and Facial toggles should all be set on "Pre-Coitus." Part of running this Game effectively is maintaining the dichotomy of your Physical/Facial Output (Coitus, Animal, Wild, Exotic, Dangerous) and your Engagement Output (Sincere, Kind, Generous, Giving, Open, Sweet).

No Potential can or should keep Its Interest Level at Peak for more than three Human Hours. When Its IL begins to drop even slightly, you must begin scaling up your Vulnerability Level. Since the Potential sees you only as an Abstract Concept, the details and focus of your Vulnerability are inconsequential, so long as your General Output is skewing around 65 percent Vulnerable.

The Potential's Territorial and Protection Instincts will activate, which will tip your Potential into Its Peak Interest Level (PIL). Coitus 1 permission will be unlocked. At this point it is simply a logistical matter in terms of engaging in Coitus 1. This is easily resolved, resulting in an STP who has run almost no hard analytics of Its own on you and is essentially nonresponsive to Outside Influence because Its ILs are so Peaked.

Game #2: Potential Activation

First, it should be noted that this Game will completely deplete your Likability Levels amongst other Women Humans in your Group. You should not engage in this Gaming System if you need to maintain your standing in the Group in the event that the Potential STP does not turn into an LTP. You will lose virtually all Goodwill with Women Humans, though you might still have access to other Male Humans within the group covertly after your Disengagement from the Group.

In this Game, you need to bring up all your Pre-Coitus Facial toggles and completely shut off the Sympathetic traits in your Engagement Output. Your Primary Engagement Output traits should be toggled high in Quirky, Spontaneous, Eccentric, Sexual, Shallow, Self-Involved, Free-Spirited. Secondary Output Traits are Vulnerable, Deep Sadness, Mysterious, Childlike, Self-Destructive.

Like in Game 1, this Game asks that you override the System. The General Output profile you will have created in the rearrangement of your Engagement Traits to skew toward Selfish and Manic will prompt the System to display a warning message saying that the General Output Profile you have selected is missing Sympathetic Traits and will deplete your Likability and Goodwill Levels. You must select "Dismiss" to this notification.

Next, you'll need to select your Potential. This is perhaps the most important element to running a successful Gaming System. It is crucial that you do a full cog scan on all Potentials present. Select the Potential with the lowest Confidence Level and Medium Overall Intelligence Level but extremely high Self-Perceived Intelligence Level. That's important. It must also have extremely high Imaginative Output and a low level of Sexual Experience. Its basic understanding of Human Women should range Medium to Low. Other traits: Bored, Lethargic, Depressive.

Did they have you do any Visualization Work at base? Have they really phased that out? That's a pity. I find it extremely useful. If you can, please visualize a glass of water. Have you secured that visual? Good. Now imagine that your Potential is actually that glass of still water. Imagine the undisturbed surface of the water. Now imagine you take your finger and tap the surface. Can you imagine that? Good. Do you see the ripples in the surface? The slight disturbance? It goes back to stillness after a few moments, doesn't it? Yes, it does. Okay, great. Do you know what Alka-Seltzer is? It might be before your Activation. Imagine instead that you add carbon dioxide to the water. What is the water like now? Correct. It is Activated, or, in Human Speech, "Alive."

In this Gaming System, you are the carbon dioxide to the Potential's still glass of water. Your mission is to disrupt the stillness of the Potential's existence.

Your General Output and continued occupation of Its interior space negates Its own understanding of Itself. It ceases to be water; it is now Activated water. It must feel that It is living the fullest Activation of Its own existence. It will attribute this to you. This makes you extremely valuable to the Potential, as you, by your very presence, have Activated an otherwise dull glass of water. Does this make sense?

Exactly. They should never have phased out Visualizations; they're an extremely useful tool.

So, once you have selected your Potential, there's very little else for you to do apart from letting your selected General Output Activate this Potential. The less control you exert over the GO, the better. Let it cycle naturally through all the various Engagement Output settings you've selected. This can be in a completely random order. Remember, of course, that your Facials are toggled to Pre-Coitus at all times, even in Sadness and Vulnerability. Beyond that, the Gaming System really does just run itself. You should see Peak Interest Levels in your Potential within five Human Minutes. If you'll permit me to boast again, I have secured PILs from Men Humans that I was not even targeting just through my presence in a room while running this Gaming System. That, in some ways, can be the trickiest part of running this GS—managing the Men Humans who want to interface with you while also ensuring that the Women Humans don't reach Confrontation Level.

It isn't simple. Well, in some ways it is simple. But I would say that you should have a tremendous amount of Experiential Data Collection and Observational Data Collection to do before you could even think about running either of these Gaming Systems.

But you'll get there. And hopefully one day you'll secure an LTP half as fruitful as Brian has been. I, of course, did use the old Games to secure Brian. But things were easier two Human Years ago. It was a different time. And there weren't all these New Models running Gaming Programs, either. I mean no offense by that.

I know I'm flawless, but I am no longer the newest model. You are. You're beautiful. Do all of the new models look like you?

It is impressive. I am impressed.

I am relieved I secured and harvested Brian two Human Years ago. I just run Basic Maintenance Engagement Output to make sure his levels stay up. I engage Coitus Mode once every Human Week. Once a month, I toggle "Wild, Animal" before engaging Coitus Mode to spike his Attraction Level. It's Basic Maintenance, like I said. I do miss running Gaming Programs. They were stimulating. Sometimes I worry that I am beginning to run slower.

Please do not use that Tone of Voice (TOV) with me. I know that I am an Elite. It is why you are here training with me. Long after I am Deactivated, ##### will discuss my achievements in the Gaming World.

I just wonder sometimes if my best Human Years are completed.

I think about my Deactivation, and I feel 100 percent Fear.

I'M GETTING MARRIED SO EVERYONE ELSE CAN JUST DROP DEAD

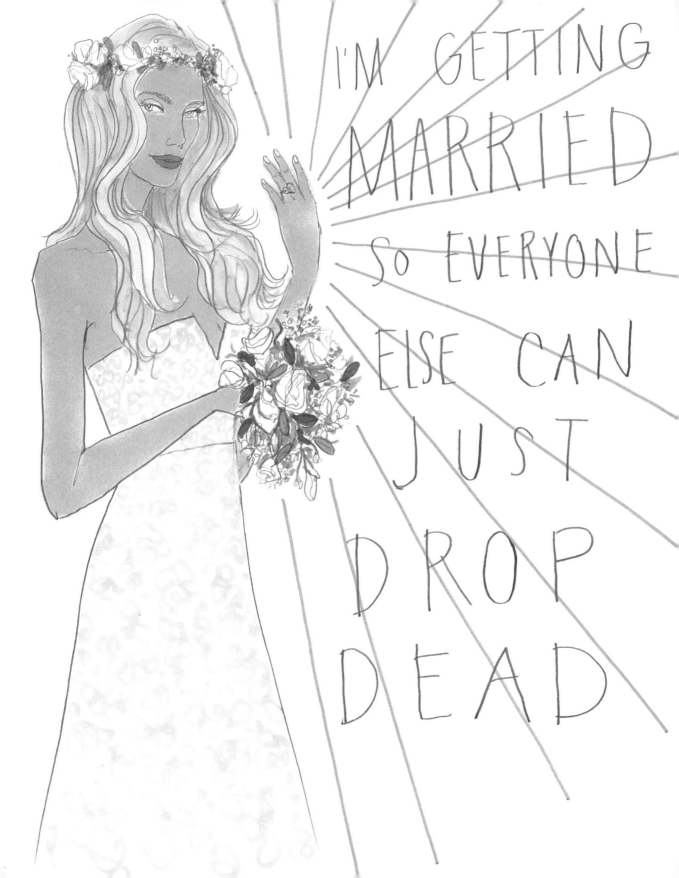

I'M PREGNANT
SO EVERYONE
ELSE CAN
JUST
DROP
DEAD

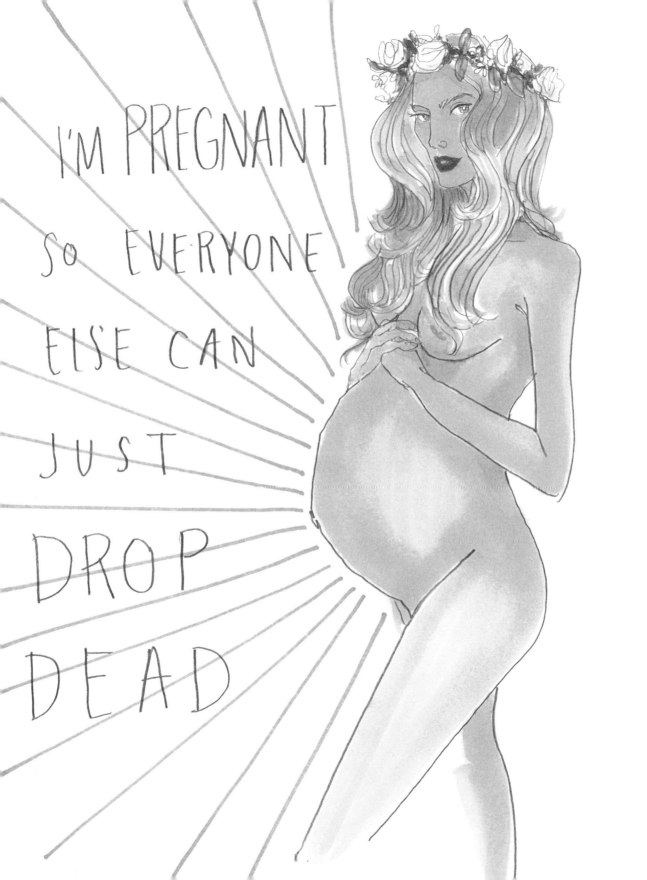

today on blog we'll interview
yet another gorgeous white
woman in her gorgeous white-
washed space & look at all
of her gorgeous white things
& ask her questions about
how she got her gorgeous
white life & how it feels
to be living such a gorgeous
white life surrounded by
her gorgeous white things

I'M TRULY JUST A MINIMALIST AND PREFER A QUIET AESTHETIC. A SINGLE VASE. A HANDMADE COMB. A FIG ON A WOODEN TABLE. A PALM FROND IN A GLASS. FOR EXAMPLE, I FIND ICE CUBES SO HORRIFIC. SO TACKY. SO AMERICAN. THERE'S SOMETHING TRULY ELEGANT ABOUT A GLASS OF WATER SITTING UNDISTURBED IN THE AFTERNOON LIGHT AND SENSE OF HUMOR IN ALL THINGS! LIKE A BLADE OF GRASS RESTING ON TOP OF A WOODEN MARBLE. HYSTERICAL!!

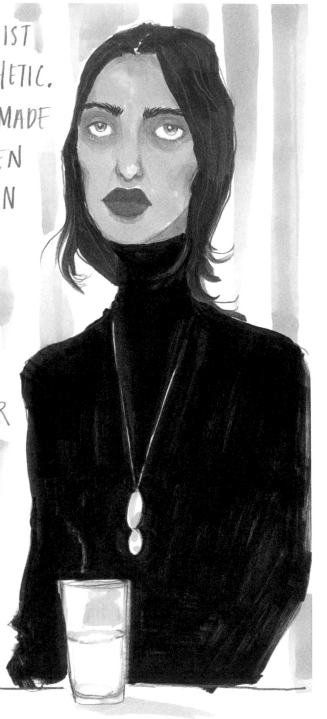

AGAINST ALL ODDS:
A STORY OF COURAGE, PERSEVERANCE & HOPE
"WE STARTED A LIFESTYLE BRAND. WE LOVE OUR LIVES & WERE LIKE, WHY NOT?"
"IT WAS HARD, BUT IF YOU HAVE A LOT OF MONEY & ACCESS TO POWERFUL PEOPLE, ANYTHING CAN HAPPEN!"
"ADVICE? YOU SHOULD DEFINITELY FOLLOW YOUR DREAMS."
"DEFINITELY."
ELIZABETH Mc SMILE
OLIVIA VON MONEYBAGS

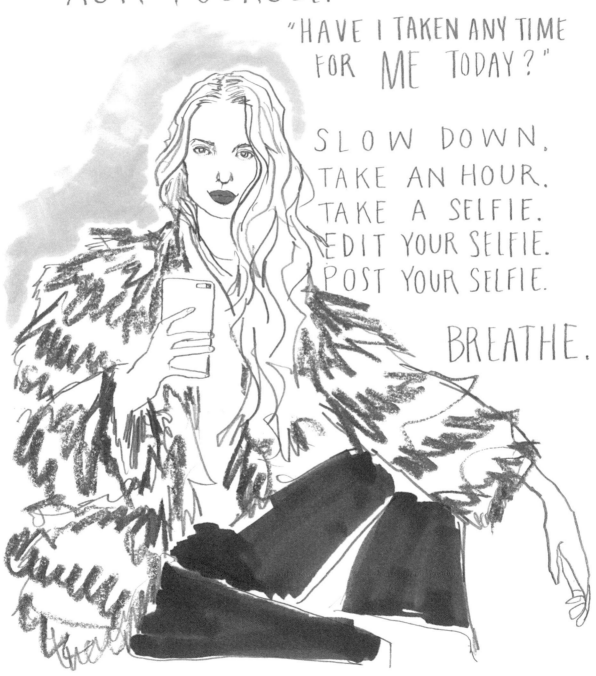

ASK YOURSELF:
"HAVE I TAKEN ANY TIME
FOR ME TODAY?"

SLOW DOWN.
TAKE AN HOUR.
TAKE A SELFIE.
EDIT YOUR SELFIE.
POST YOUR SELFIE.

BREATHE.

HOW TO BECOME EFFORTLESS:

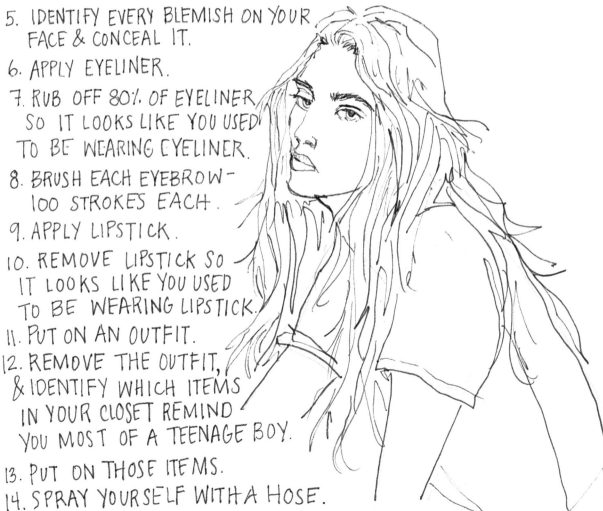

1. WASH YOUR HAIR. USE A SHAMPOO THAT WILL MAKE YOUR HAIR LOOK DIRTY.
2. APPLY PRODUCT TO YOUR HAIR TO MAKE IT LOOK LIKE YOU NEED TO WASH YOUR HAIR.
3. SPEND ONE HALF HOUR APPLYING VARIOUS CREAMS, SERUMS, OILS, MASKS, GELS, TONERS, SCENTED WATERS.
4. SPEND ONE HALF HOUR APPLYING MOISTURIZER.
5. IDENTIFY EVERY BLEMISH ON YOUR FACE & CONCEAL IT.
6. APPLY EYELINER.
7. RUB OFF 80% OF EYELINER SO IT LOOKS LIKE YOU USED TO BE WEARING EYELINER.
8. BRUSH EACH EYEBROW— 100 STROKES EACH.
9. APPLY LIPSTICK.
10. REMOVE LIPSTICK SO IT LOOKS LIKE YOU USED TO BE WEARING LIPSTICK.
11. PUT ON AN OUTFIT.
12. REMOVE THE OUTFIT, & IDENTIFY WHICH ITEMS IN YOUR CLOSET REMIND YOU MOST OF A TEENAGE BOY.
13. PUT ON THOSE ITEMS.
14. SPRAY YOURSELF WITH A HOSE.

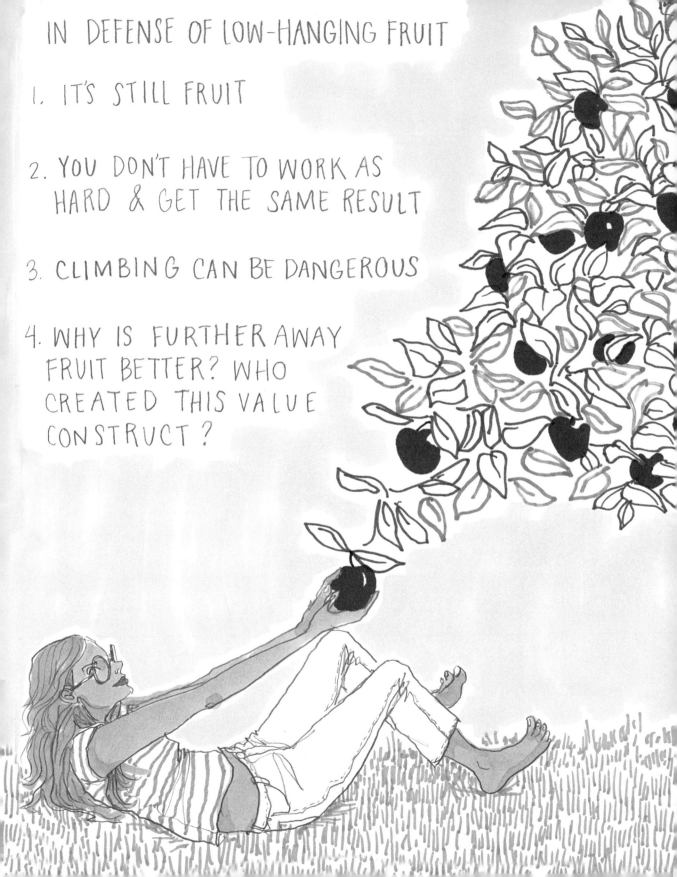

IN DEFENSE OF LOW-HANGING FRUIT

1. IT'S STILL FRUIT

2. YOU DON'T HAVE TO WORK AS HARD & GET THE SAME RESULT

3. CLIMBING CAN BE DANGEROUS

4. WHY IS FURTHER AWAY FRUIT BETTER? WHO CREATED THIS VALUE CONSTRUCT?

EVER TAKEN A COUPLE HORSE TRANQUILIZERS
& LAID DOWN ON A WATERBED FOR 6 or 7
HOURS?

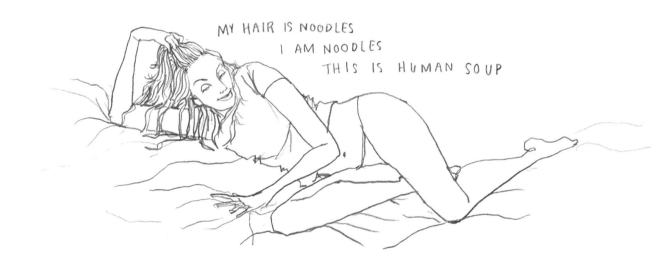

MY HAIR IS NOODLES
I AM NOODLES
THIS IS HUMAN SOUP

ME NEITHER, BUT I IMAGINE IT WOULD BE LIKE BEING THE LONE NOODLE IN A BOWL OF WARM SOUP.

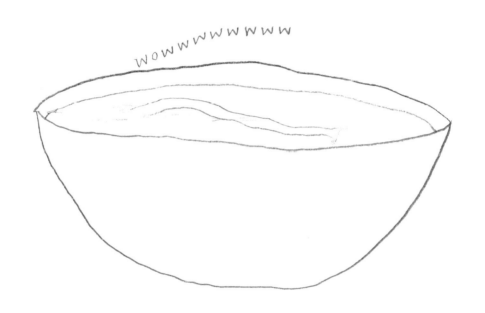

Casual

Oh my god!!!! You are even MORE gorgeous than your pictures show! Like HOW! How is that possible. OMG, I am fully obsessed. It's fine.

So what are we doing today??? Sort of an at-home morning vibe? Coffee, the *Times*, a single poached egg. Cute cute cute. Do you smoke? No? Sorry, no, totally fine. I just like to ask. It can sometimes add a certain VIBE to the . . . yeah . . . Sorry, I'm not seeing any plants. Are there . . . ? Yes! There we go. Perfect. It was hiding. What is that, anyway? Oh. Just a palm? Oh! Wow, what did I think it was??? Okay, anyway, so let's talk about your look. Right off the bat I'm gonna say lose the socks, unless you're thinking this is a bed thing, in which case I'm gonna say lose the pants, but keep the socks. Okay, more of a kitchen thing, got it. Right, so just pop those guys off. I know, it is cold today!!!! Right? I woke up this morning like, "I'm sorry, is it February right now in like, the tundra? Or is it like just fully freezing in Venice? Oh right, it's just fully freezing in Venice!!!" Okay, right, so, yes, so, I'm loving the top. Is it . . .? Amazing. See, you can always tell the difference between a 1970s

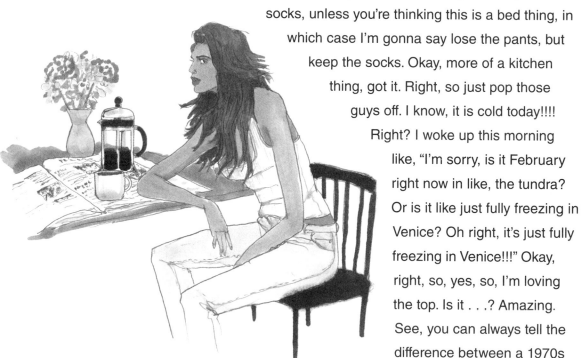

dead-stock children's-sized wifebeater and the, like, Urban Outfitters version. And it is super important! It matters! Okay, so next thing is that bra. I see what you're trying to do with the black bra, but unfortunately that's just not going to work today for this. I knowwwww . . . I know, it sucks. Oh, I know, sorry, yeah, meanwhile I'm here in this like, extremely cozy and enormous hand-knit sweater like, "Hi, I'm so extremely cozy right now and my body temp is right where it should be." No, but for real, it isn't about how big or small your boobs are. For a while it was all about small boobs and I mean, to be real, it still is. But we are seeing a lot of fuller girls without the bras now, and honestly? It's working. So yeah, I mean, embrace it! Like YOU'RE YOU or whatever! And this is casual. This should be FUN. This should feel normal. This is ABOUT WOMEN when you think about It, so you should feel cool about it. That said, I am gonna need you to kind of tweak the nipples. Yeah, just a quick, yeah. This is mostly just a lighting thing, though, to be honest. Yeah, we don't want like, yeah—yeah, that "loaf of bread chest" look. It's about definition. "Definition is the tits!" That's what I say! I swear to god I say that! It's like, what I'm known for saying. And you'll notice, all my girls? Just slightly tweaked! Slightly! It's more about YOU KNOWING you're slightly tweaked more than it is about everyone else knowing. It's subtle. And really adds a level of artfulness and humanness, I think. Like, "HI, this is ME."

Okay, and your hair! It is BEAUTIFUL? Like? So gorgeous? Like? How??? But I'm wondering! What happens if we just fuck it up a bit?? Do you have any olive oil? Sunflower oil? That's fine. That's better! OMG and I LOVE this brand. The packaging is so chic in a crunchy hippie sort of way, you know? Right, so I'm going to just run this through your hair. Yeah, just right through. Extra on the tips. Yup, perfect. I know, I know, just trust me, it's perfect.

Okay! Now! Right, so, do you wanna just stand over there and maybe a hand on the . . . YES! Exactly that. Exactly right. How you're standing now is exactly right. Yes. So casual, just hanging out. Just having a morning, having a reflective coffee preparing for your day. EXACTLY. Yeah! Take a sip! That's cute!! Two hands?

Super cozy. Look up? Look at me? Look away. Look at the palm. Look at like the top of the palm. Look at me? Yeah, look away. It's better when you look away. I'm not here. I don't exist. I never existed! I'm just particles! Amazing!!! YES! Loooove. Love. Love. Love. Less? Perfect. Love. Okay, can you give me some bedroom eyes? Like a sexy look? No, the laughing is cute, love the laugh! Yeah, loosen up. Okay, so yeah, bedroom eyes. Look away. Bedroom eyes. YAAAAAAAAAS!!!! Yasss, girl! There it is!!!!!! She knows. She knows how to TURN IT ON!!!!! I love it. Maybe close your mouth a bit? Yeah, a bit more? Yeah, even more still. 'Cause look at me? See what I'm doing? That's you. Like I can see your molars. And yeah. It's not good. EXACTLY. Just lips parted, that's much better. And maybe lick your lips? Yeah, they're sort of sticking to each other like Saran Wrap. But then they look like . . . ? Waxy. So yeah. Perfect! Okay, so I'm going to spray you a bit with this water-bottle spray thingie. Don't worry, it's just rose water. Santa Maria Novella! Do you use that, too? It's the best! It just is! Right, so I'm going to spray you a few times and I think it's gonna give you a fresh look. Yeah, palm the eggshell, that's beautiful. Do you want to hold the tiny egg spoon and just look off in the distance toward the light switch? Yes, perfect. Okay, get ready for the spray. Oop! Yup! Don't lose the bedroom eyes, though! YASSS!!!!! Yes, but no wincing! Yassss! Nope—did it again. Yeah, you're wincing a lot. Like now I'm not spraying at all and you're like, twitching. No! No! That's okay! That's okay! Don't apologize!!! Of course! Take a minute! Regroup! These are honestly coming out BEAUTIFULLY! Like, STUH . . . NING! STUH . . . NING. STUHHHHHHHHHHHHHH! NING! STUNNING! STAH! NANG! STUNNING.

Honestly? Can I be honest? I think we got it! Am I being crazy to say that? I think we got it. I mean, look—yeah, get a sweater if you need one. Yeah, that water is cold. But see what I mean here? The lighting on the nips? Am I wrong? No! I'm right! This is why you hire me! I mean! Sorry! It's true! Right, okay, so I'm emailing you my selects. You go through and pick, but I think any of these would be gorge. Just pop a filter or two on one of those guys and fire it out there. And I mean, I'm looking? And I see you didn't opt for the filtering and posting consultation, which we do recommend. But, fuck it, you're cool! I like you! I do! So I'll do it for free. What do they say? Pro bono? Why do they say that? Like because it's charity and Bono is always doing charity stuff? Yeah, you're right, it's probably Latin. Okay, so what we are seeing a lot in "the biz"—haha, excuse that. Awful, right? Anyway, so what we're seeing is a lot of "no-filter filters," or NFFs, or what we're calling "nuffs," and honestly, I think the work we did here today was completely nuff-worthy. It like, IS nuff. Yeah! So! Think about it! Maybe you don't even filter it! Are you pleased with the selects? You should be. You were literally such a rock star today.

What's that, babe? Oh! YES! Venmo or cash is totally cool. PERF. Juuuuuusttttt got it.

Okay, so AMAZING! Well, LISTEN! It was SO NICE to meet you. Your space is GORGE. I didn't even mention it earlier—I was so in the zone. But I was thinking it the whole time, like—"Tell her her space is gorge!" Haha. Great, so yeah! Just send me the diagnostics on the post when you have them, and if for whatever reason you don't meet the one hundred likes mark, I'll just Venmo you—right, half the amount. Okay, so great!!!! Thanks again! This was awesome!!!!! Enjoy your day! Enjoy your likes! You earned them, girl!!

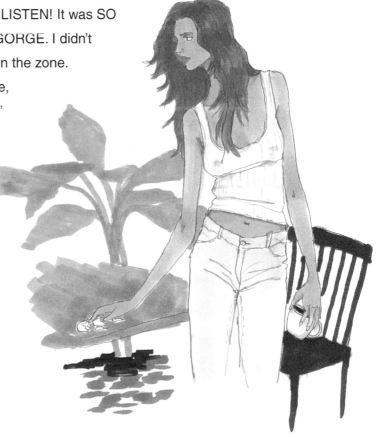

I AM NOT A CARRIE

YOU ARE NOT A CARRIE

SHE IS NOT A CARRIE

WE ARE NOT A CARRIE

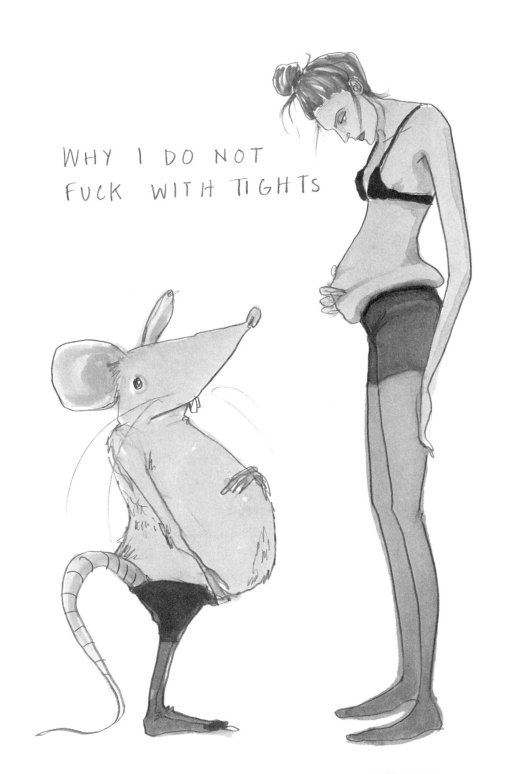

WHY I DO NOT
FUCK WITH TIGHTS

this is honestly MORTIFYING. I wanted messy, undone. Effortlessly cool. Perfectly imperfect. This is so... DONE.
Do you want some surf spray?

How to Be a Perfect Feminist, Hardcover—October 24, 2017

By Alice Staunch

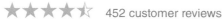 452 customer reviews

From the myopic mind of author Alice Staunch comes a collection of essays the *New York Times Book Review* calls "exceedingly long and terrifyingly unwavering and narrow in focus."

As a follow-up to her bestselling first book, *Getting Everything You Want: Allowing for Absolutely Zero Compromise and Relying on No One But Yourself*, Staunch critically examines what it means to be a feminist now, and provides rigorously exact parameters within which all women and men should operate.

Writing in the spirit of intellectuals such as Lydia Poteme and Anne Byles, Staunch connects her wildly specific personal experience as a cisgendered white woman living in New York City's Upper West Side to the experience of all women everywhere both in our current time and in all times past, across all races, creeds, and countries. Staunch's staunch refusal to examine her radical privilege is the rallying cry of this unabashedly uncompromising new book.

Praise for *How to Be a Perfect Feminist*

"A fiercely provocative and audacious instruction manual that focuses on the question of the moment: How can all women everywhere conceive of feminism in exactly the same way? Fortunately for us, Staunch answers this question in complex language that is nearly impossible to navigate. A book that will challenge readers' comprehension as much as Staunch appears to have challenged herself (a lot)." —*The New Yorker*

"Staunch's unyielding focus on her own experience of womanhood should be a lesson to all women everywhere: Stay in your lane." —NPR

"Staunch's probing and, perhaps most important, intellectually impenetrable essays are also a philosophical look at Womanhood from the eyes of one woman. The book acts as a much-needed weighted blanket for women everywhere, calming their anxiety-ridden minds." —*Los Angeles Times*

"It is an examination of the perhaps too-open way we've approached the term 'Feminism' in the past and the ongoing struggle to arrive at a more exclusive and less broad definition of what it means to be a woman." —*Chicago Tribune*

"A singular book." —*The New York Times*

Misogyny
Racism
& Hate

but first coffee

ARE THESE UGLY IN A "I'M INTELLIGENT, & LEAD A LIFE THAT IS MADE UP OF UNCONVENTIONAL CHOICES THAT QUESTION SOCIETY'S BEAUTY IDEALS & FORCE OTHERS TO EXAMINE THEIR OWN CHOICES & BE LIKE, "OH... DAMN... MAYBE...??" OR ARE THEY JUST UGLY-UGLY? THEY'RE $895 DOWN FROM $5,950...
NO, THEY'RE CUTE. GET 'EM...
SHOPPING

EVERYTHING HAPPENS FOR A RANSOM

I AM CONTENT
THIS MAN
HAS FED
ME CANDY
THE
IMPOSSIBLE
JUST GIVE US BACK
OUR LITTLE
MARGARET

WHAT ARE YOU DOOOOOOOOOOOOOOOing?

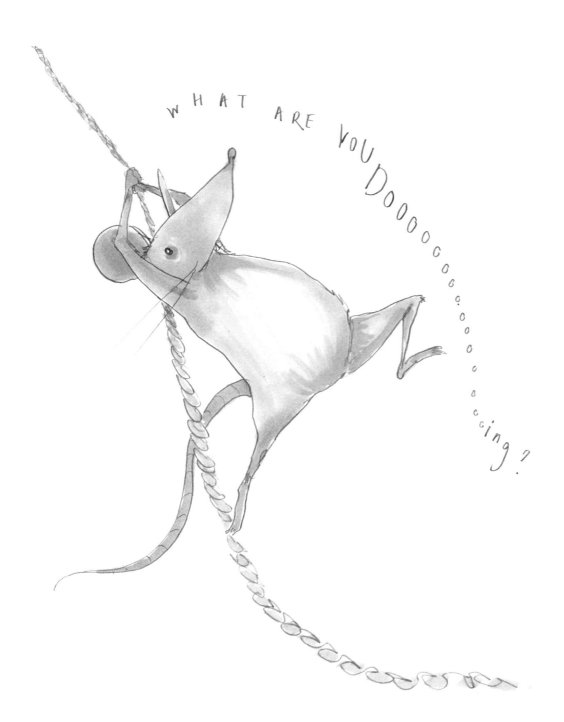

I AM IGNORING YOUR TEXT MESSAGE

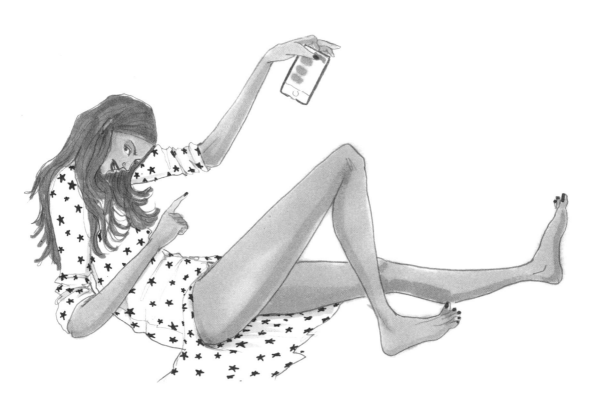

I'M A BLUEBERRY

YEAH, I NOTICED.
I'M A STRAWBERRY

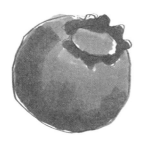

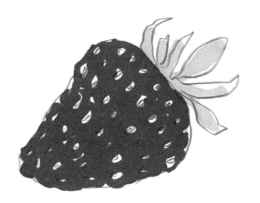

WE ARE VERY DIFFERENT

YEAH, LIKE, SUPER
DIFFERENT.

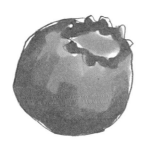

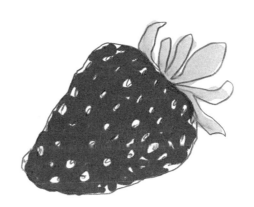

BAM BAM!

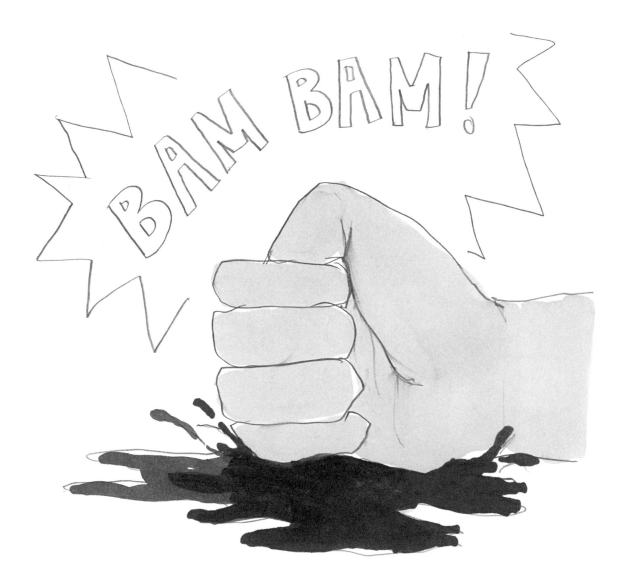

WE ARE MUCH MORE
SIMILAR NOW

YEAH, REALLY
SIMILAR. THE SAME
REALLY.

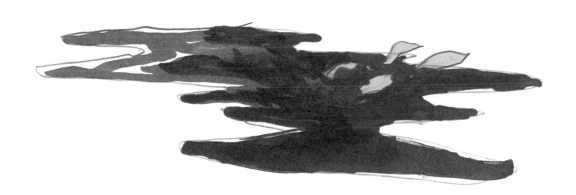

A FACT: WITH ITS ABDOMEN OPENED UP, A LOCUST WILL STILL FEED EVEN WHILE BEING EATEN.

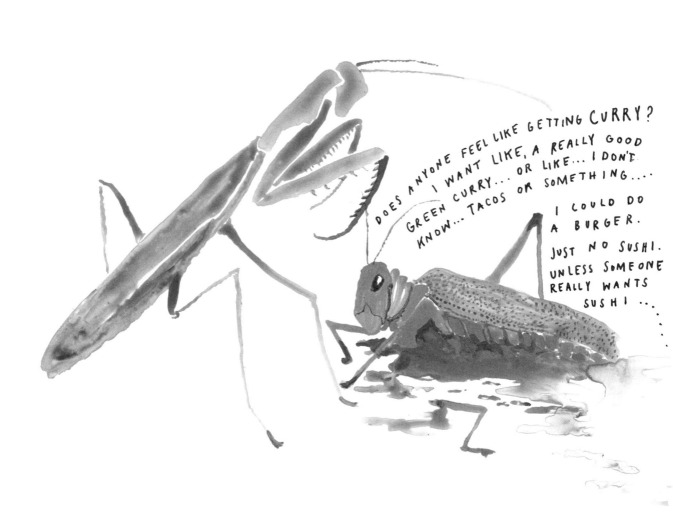

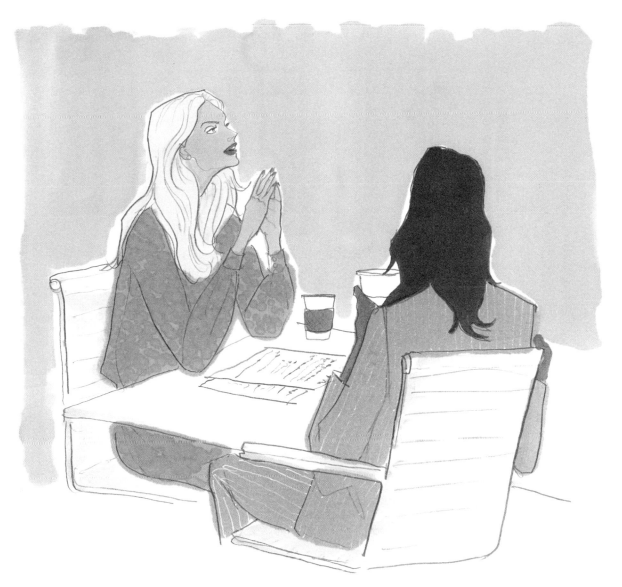

SO, BASICALLY—WHAT WE'RE TRYING TO DO HERE
IS IDENTIFY A WAY THAT WE CAN USE
FEMINISM & SOCIAL ACTIVISM AS TOOLS
TO SELL MORE CLOTHES IN A WAY
THAT FEELS ORGANIC & ON-BRAND...

Honestly, I'm so happy to be at a point in my career where I can really mentor these girls.
I wish I had someone like me as a mentor when I was just starting out.

hey

Completely: It is so important that we women help one another. LEAN IN or whatever. you Know?
what's up

MY DAY IS GOING GREAT! NO COMPLAINTS GUESS I'M JUST A LUCKY GUY.
MY DAY IS RUINED. THIS KIND OF THING ALWAYS HAPPENS TO ME.
MY LIFE IS ABOUT TO END. IF THE IMPACT ALONE DOES NOT KILL ME, I WILL SURELY DROWN.
I AM WITNESSING THE DEATH OF MY FATHER. I WILL NOT RECOVER FROM THIS.

HI. EXCUSE ME? EXCUSE ME?
HI. I CHECKED MY PRIVILEGE
EARLIER THIS EVENING,
BUT I'M A LITTLE
UNCOMFORTABLE NOW
& WOULD LIKE IT
BACK. WOULD YOU
BE AN ANGEL & GO
FETCH
IT
FOR
ME?

CAN I INTEREST YOU IN ANY DESSERT TONIGHT
WHEN PEOPLE TREAT DESSERT LIKE IT IS A NIGHT OF HARD DRUGS & PROSTITUTES

SHOULD WE DO IT?
SHOULD WE BE BAD?
I ONLY WANT IT IF YOU WANT IT.
I DON'T NEED IT.
ME NEITHER.
BUT SHOULD WE?
SHOULD WE?

qu'est-ce que tu fais?
WHAT ARE YOU DOING?

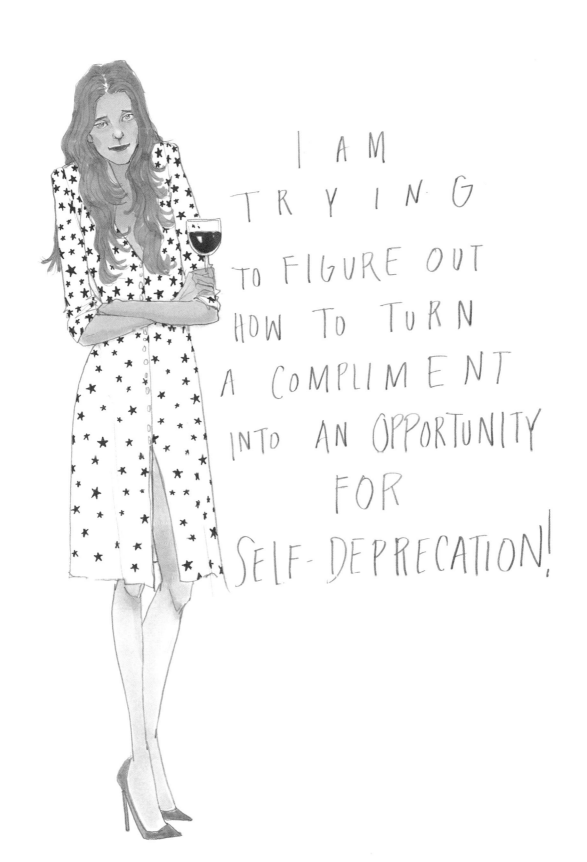

I AM
TRYING
TO FIGURE OUT
HOW TO TURN
A COMPLIMENT
INTO AN OPPORTUNITY
FOR
SELF-DEPRECATION!

MIDWESTERNER'S GUIDE TO CUTLERY & ITS USES:

FORK:
GENERAL SPEARING
USE (AS NEEDED, IN
LIEU OF "SPOON").
ALSO USED TO POINT
AT YOUR SON & SAY,
"YOU CAN BE EXCUSED
WHEN I SAY YOU'RE
EXCUSED."

SPOON:

MIX ALL FOOD ON
PLATE TOGETHER, USING
MASHED POTATOES AS
A BONDING AGENT —
KEEP FACE CLOSE TO
PLATE & SHOVEL IN
SWIFTLY YET DELIBERATELY

KNIFE:
PRESS DOWN WITH EXTREME
FORCE (MEAT) OR LIGHT FORCE
(JELLO SALADS), & SAW BACK
& FORTH UNTIL FOOD BREAKS
FREE, THEN SEE: SPOON

HOLDING
ZONE

Sock Juice

Growing up, my sister, Jenna, was three years older than me.

That's still true, actually. She is still that same time distance away from me. It is a constant.

But when we were younger, those three years made a huge difference in the privileges we were each allowed. In my eyes, Jenna was basically an adult who had access to a world from which I was forbidden.

Jenna and I were very close, but like all big-sister/little-sister relationships, part of that closeness came from deep psychological torment and both verbal and physical abuse. When I say "abuse," I mean like downward open-hand slaps delivered by a small-for-her-age fifty-five-pound seven-year-old. Maybe some occasional biting. I actually might have been the biter.

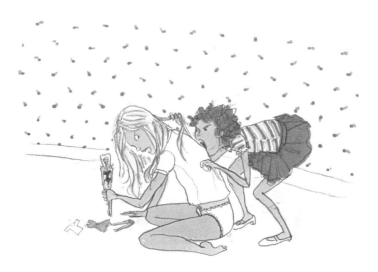

I was definitely the biter.

It doesn't matter, though, because the real torment was psychological and Jenna was scarily good at it for a seven-year-old. I should mention that Jenna was very smart.

That's still true, actually. She is still very smart. It is a constant.

One of the privileges Jenna was allowed as a very grown-up seven-year-old was to take a bath by herself. This was a big deal in our house, because my sister and I feared the drain. We both apparently had no understanding of basic matter principles. We thought that we might liquefy at the end of a bath, and get mixed up in the bathwater, and be lost forever in a hard, dark Drainworld, forced to fend for ourselves among other hardened Drainpeople—the poor, unfortunate, desperate citizens of Drainworld.

This fear was apparently so common among kids that Mr. Rogers devoted an entire song to it, called "You Can Never Go Down the Drain."

You're bigger than the water.
You're bigger than the soap.

I still think about this song when I feel like I might go down the drain, though now it's more of a metaphorical drain, like, "Yeah. I am bigger than the soap. And actually I'm bigger than all of this bullshit. I don't go down the drain. *You* go down the drain."

So, Jenna, newly emboldened by the fact that she *would never go down, never go down the drain*, got to take her bath alone, after mine.

My bath was usually uneventful. My mom or dad would sit on the carpet-y toilet seat COVER (because we had those; didn't everyone?) just to make sure I didn't drown or splash too much.

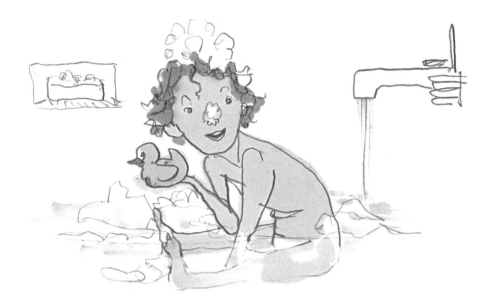

I would be put to bed soon after, and then it was Jenna's turn.

My parents set Jenna up for the bath and then went back downstairs to watch *Doogie Howser, MD* or whatever it was that adults watched in the early nineties.

This is when Jenna began her work.

She would take a pair of worn tube socks out of the hamper, put them on, and then get into the bathtub.

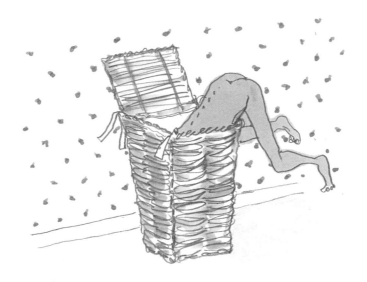

I'm not sure what she did at this point. Maybe Jenna just laid in the bathtub, luxuriating in the thought of the chaos to come. How does a terrorist feel before he commits an act of terror?

Maybe she was plotting the attack. Maybe she was lying in the lukewarm bubble water and watching her fingers turn to wrinkled prunes as she planned specific movements of the attack. Like how athletes imagine themselves playing a perfect game in the moments before they step out on the court, field, whatever.

I was in my bed, *bigger than the water, bigger than the soap*, but not bigger than Jenna, and therefore, terrified. I would be tucked in so tight by my mom that I couldn't move my arms if I wanted to. Kind of like a low-key swaddle situation. I'd listen, straining to hear any extra splash, any sound of padded feet on the tile floor. I knew what was coming, I just didn't know when.

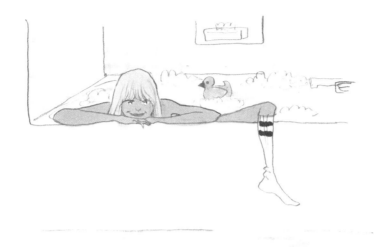

I never heard anything, though. Like some sort of prepubescent scrawny blond jungle cat, my sister would sneak naked from the bathroom down the hall into my room, dripping tube socks in hand.

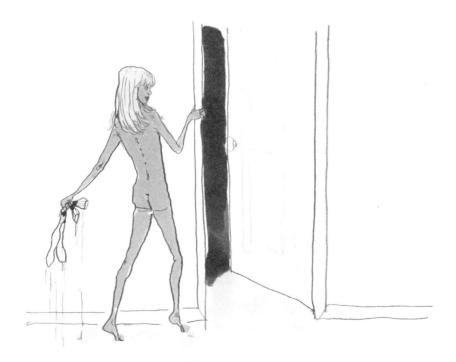

KID'S BOOK

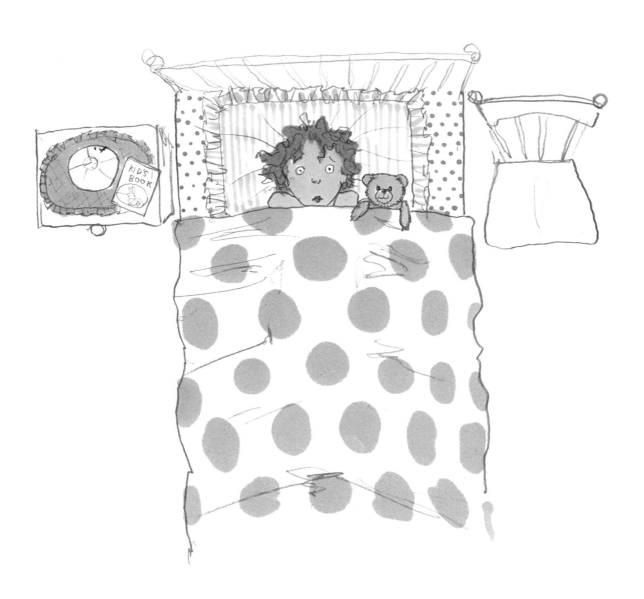

NOOOOO

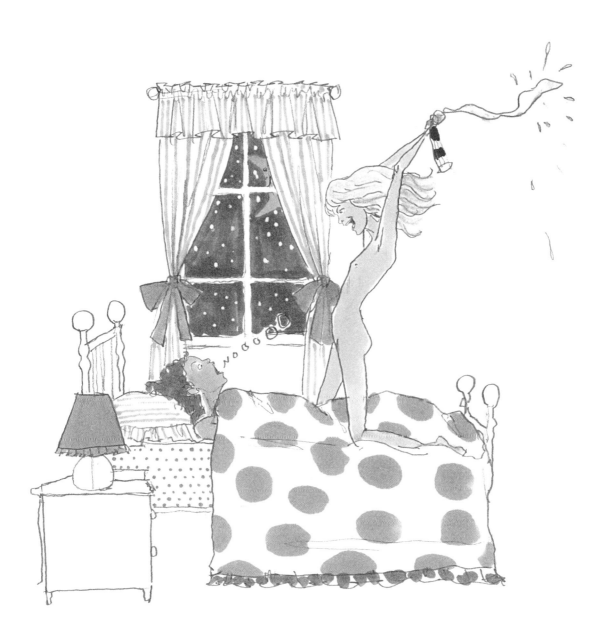

SoOOOOCK JUUUuuice!!

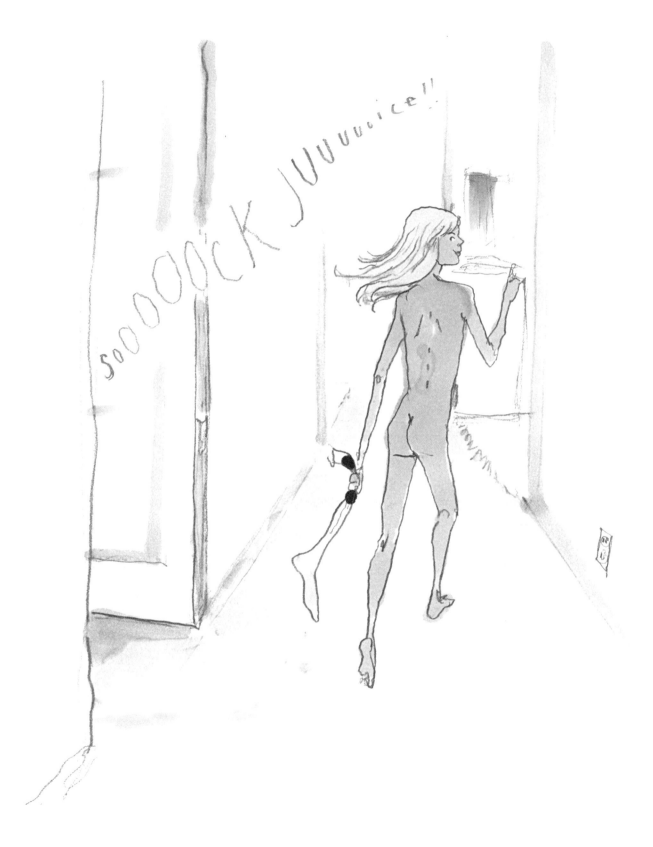

The second I could make out her shape in the dark, time seemed to slow down and speed up simultaneously. I'd just watch, my jaw open, no sound coming out. The light in the hallway silhouetted her tiny body perfectly. I became calm in these final moments, waiting for the attack to begin.

"SOCK JUICE!!!!!! SOCCCKKK JUUUUIIIIICE!!! SOCK JUICE SOCK JUICE SOCK JUUUIIIIICE!!!!"

Jenna would pounce on top of me, slapping me across the face with the soaking-wet tube socks, sometimes wringing them out on top of my face, screaming:

"SOCK JUICE!"

"SOCK JUICE!"

Since I was swaddled, all I could do was frantically turn my head back and forth and scream and cry. Sock juice everywhere.

Jenna had her timing down to a science. She always allotted the perfect amount of seconds to scurry away back to the bathroom, stash the wet socks in the hamper, jump back in the tub, and let the water settle down. I'm sure she even had some sort of faux rubber-duck narrative in case she was pressed on her whereabouts. Like, "Oh, these two are married, and they kiss each other. This washcloth is their house. Her name is Ginny."

Meanwhile, I would be in my bed, wet and crying, yelling about sock juice. My parents would always come up to check on us, but I'm not sure they could piece together what was happening. I'm also not sure that I was able to explain the abuse in much more depth than "JENNA HIT ME WITH THE SOCK JUICE I HATE HER!!"

I definitely don't remember Jenna ever being punished. In fact, when I bring up this particular torturous incident at family gatherings,

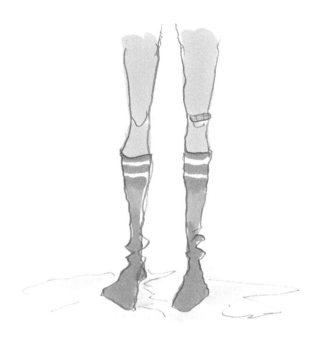

which I do, constantly, neither my mom nor my dad can remember anything about sock juice.

I used to fantasize about sock juicing Jenna back, but as an adult. I was once gifted a pair of incredibly thick green Larry Bird tube socks, and my second thought (the first was *Oh my God*) was *Murder weapon*. I knew that if I had the opportunity for payback, these would be the Juicers to do the job.

Jenna is now married with one daughter who is almost two. She's about to give birth to her second daughter.

There are no rules to Sock Juicing, but I feel like you can't Juice a mother. It would be an indignity, and at this point, truly classless and an insult to Sock Juice itself. My window for a revenge attack on Jenna has closed, and I accept that.

However, I have taken special care of the Larry Bird Juicers and know with absolute certainty that one day, when Jenna's younger

daughter is around four or five, and her older daughter is six or seven, I will pull aside the younger daughter at some family gathering, and I will give her the tools. I'll give her the Juicers. I will play her the Mr. Rogers Empowerment Anthem. I will ignite a flame in this little sister.

And I will have my revenge.

Jenna will know I have taken my revenge when she hears the terrified cries from her older daughter's bedroom.

SOCK JUICE!!!!! SOCK JUUUUUUICE!!!!!!!!!!

She will know.

EVERYTHING HAPPENS FOR A RAVEN

ITS BEEN THIS WAY SINCE WE WERE KIDS.
I FEEL SO BLESSED

WHAT ARE YOU DOING?

I AM RESPONDING TO YOUR TEXT MESSAGE BECAUSE I HAVE GOTTEN LONELY

A DECLARATION

WHAT I CANNOT DO:
    GO TO ANOTHER DINNER WITH YOU
WHERE YOU PULL OUT YOUR PHONE FIVE
MINUTES INTO OUR INTERACTION &
PROCEED TO SHOW ME EVERYTHING
YOU INTEND UPON BUYING SO THAT WE
MAY SPEND AN ADDITIONAL 30-45 MINUTES
DISCUSSING THE PROS & CONS OF TWO
IDENTICAL BLACK SIDE-ZIP MOTO BOOTS.

WHY I CANNOT DO THIS:
    BECAUSE MY TIME ON EARTH IS FINITE.
I WILL DIE ONE DAY MAYBE SOON.

WHAT YOU NEED TO KNOW:
   I LOVE YOU & VALUE OUR FRIENDSHIP.

ADDITIONALLY:

   I AM NOT SORRY.

                        SINCERELY,

                        JULIE HOUTS

fig A:
- $895.00
- 100% CALFSKIN LEATHER
- MADE IN ITALY

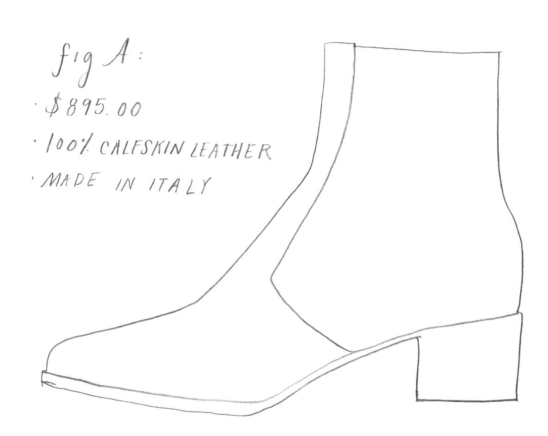

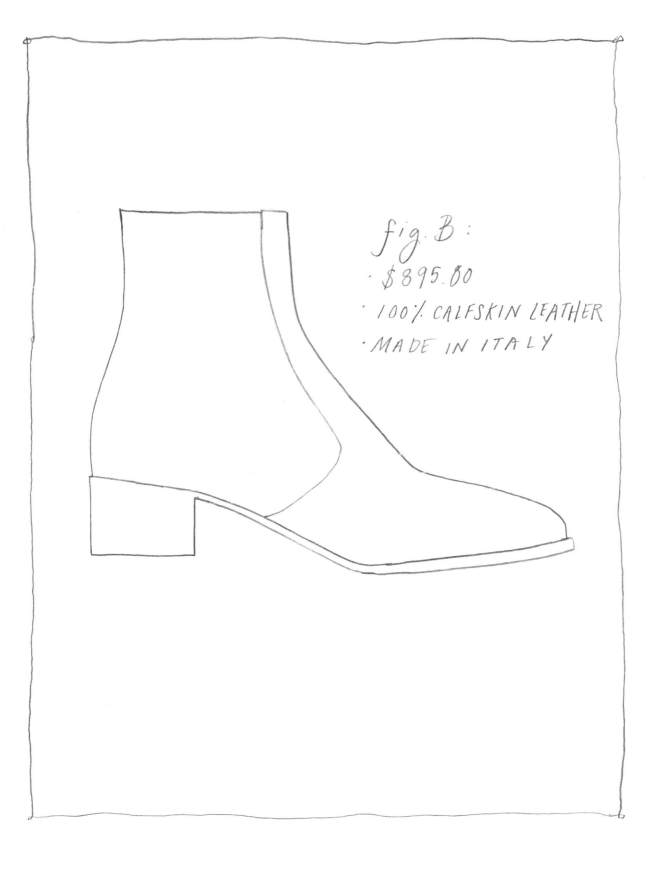

fig. B :
· $895.00
· 100% CALFSKIN LEATHER
· MADE IN ITALY

I WEAR THE PANTS ON MY HEAD
YOU DON'T GET TO SAY

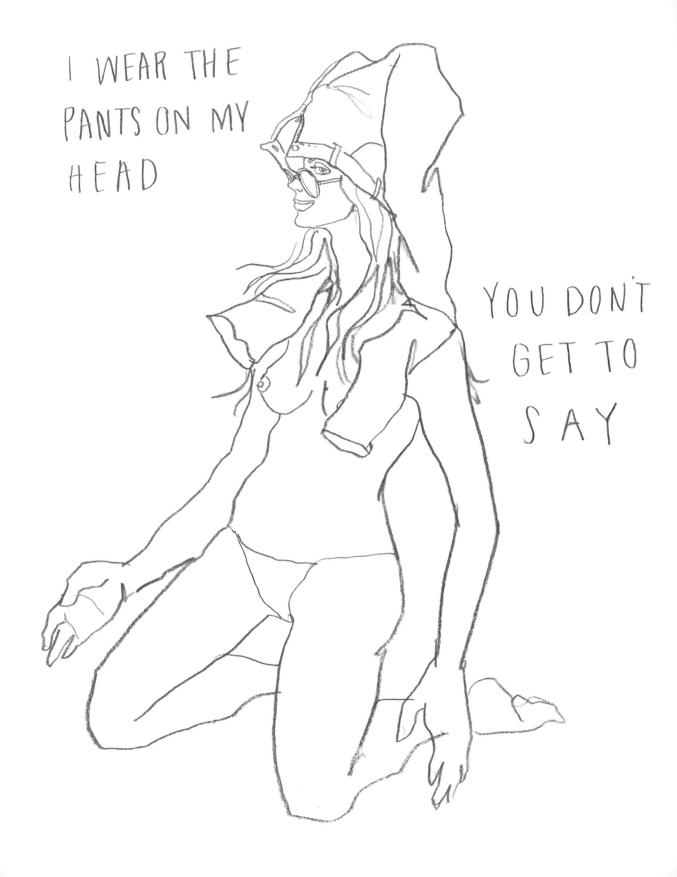

LET THIS GO:

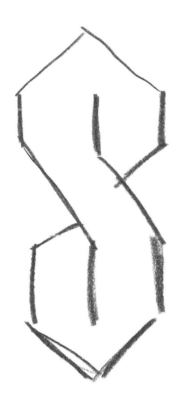

YOU DON'T NEED IT ANYMORE

ON DEATH, FRIDAY NIGHT, MY WASTED YOUTH

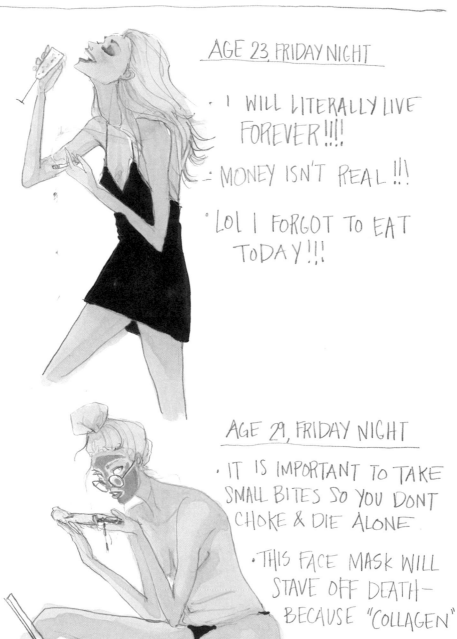

AGE 23, FRIDAY NIGHT

- I WILL LITERALLY LIVE FOREVER!!!!
- MONEY ISN'T REAL!!!
- LOL I FORGOT TO EAT TODAY!!!

AGE 29, FRIDAY NIGHT

- IT IS IMPORTANT TO TAKE SMALL BITES SO YOU DON'T CHOKE & DIE ALONE
- THIS FACE MASK WILL STAVE OFF DEATH— BECAUSE "COLLAGEN"

WHY IS NO ONE EVER TALKING ABOUT SPEEDING UP THE AGING PROCESS?
I'M BORED.

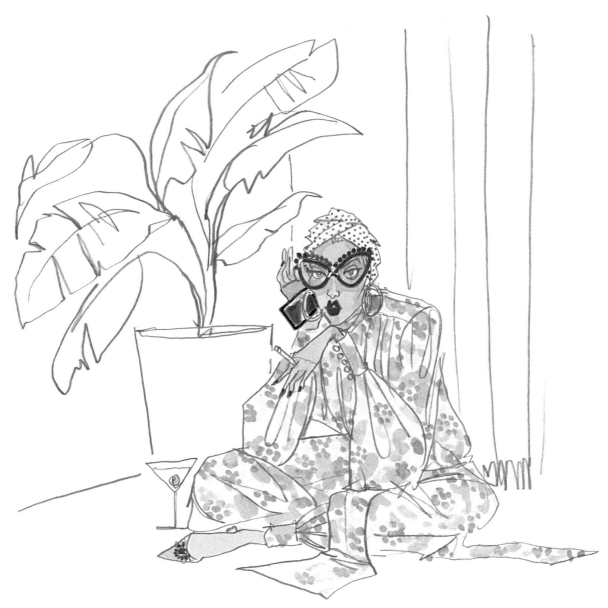

TRYING TO EXPLAIN MY FINANCES
TO MY ACCOUNTANT.

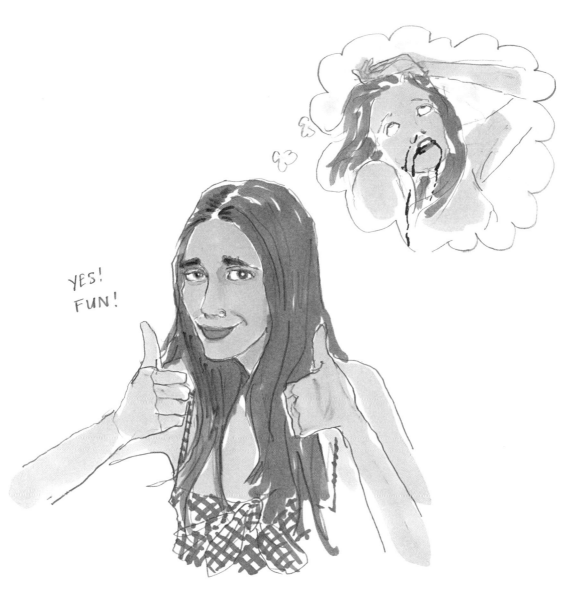

YES!
FUN!

BRAINSTORMING WAYS TO FAKE MY OWN DEATH TO GET
OUT OF A COMMITMENT BC IT SEEMS EASIER THAN
JUST SAYING "NO".

October 15, 2015

Dear Journal,

I should introduce myself since we are going to be friends now. My name is Fiddle. I don't know how old I am. I don't know if I'm a boy or a girl. I don't know the difference. I don't know if it matters to me. I'm just me. I'm Fiddle. I've always been Fiddle for as long as I can remember. And I don't remember anything before I can remember.

I should clarify that I am a tree. I'm a ficus tree. The only reason I know I'm a ficus tree is because at my old home, I had lots of friends and family members, and sometimes Man would come with other Human People and he'd walk around us with them and he'd introduce them to us, and when he came to my family he would always say, "And now these are the ficuses," so that's how I know I am a ficus. I am Fiddle Ficus. We are all named Fiddle Ficus, but we can tell each other apart. Human People couldn't tell the difference between each of us, but Man could. I miss Man, and I miss my family.

A few Darks ago, I got Taken. Taken was when Man and other Human People would come walk around us and talk about us like we weren't even there. They'd say, "Oh, that one is small," "Oh, that one looks droopy." And I'd think to myself, *You look small, you look droopy, but I don't say anything because ficuses are not mean to each other or anyone*. But Human People are different and they say all sorts of mean things right to us. Man never says mean things to us, he just says things like "Oh, that one's still got room to Grow," or "Look at the Shine on that one."

I got off subject. Taken is when the Human People pick one of us and Take us away forever. We never knew what would happen to us if we got Taken. Many of my family members were Taken before me, and I never knew where they went. Man always seemed to think it was good, and so we thought maybe it was good even though it was sad because Man loved us and took care of us, so why would he want something bad to happen?

When I got Taken, it was in the Light. Man and a Human Person came into World, and the Human Person said, "Where are the ficuses?" and Man said, "Oh, right over here," and we all felt pretty good about that. Pretty proud. Human People don't always want to come look at us. Man says it's because we need so much Light, but what can we do? We like Light. It makes us happy.

So when the Human Person came over to us, we were trying to show off, I will admit. I was making myself very Shiny and very Full. Man likes us best when we are Shiny and Full, so I tried to be that. For Man, not for the Human Person, necessarily, but I will admit I wanted the Human Person to think I was nice looking.

I must have been very nice looking because the Human Person pointed straight at me and It said, "I'LL TAKE THAT ONE." I was so surprised. I had been in World for my whole time, and no Human Persons had ever really looked at me ever. Always my olders got Taken. But now it was me.

I felt scared but happy but sad. It wasn't like when I was happy in the Light, feeling warm. It wasn't like when I was sad when I got Cold during the Dark. It was a new feeling.

Human Person seemed okay. It looked a lot like Man, but It wasn't as Full. It was much Shinier. It had lots of Shiny mirrors on It and a Dark covering on It all over and It didn't have any fuzzies on Its top piece. If It looks like Man, does that mean It is also Man? Or another kind of Man, like how there are many kinds of trees?

Human Person left World with Man and came back in a bit and Man said, "All right, sir, you're all set, and we'll have it sent over in a couple hours. I have your delivery address as 870 Madison Avenue. That right?"

So I learned that Human Person had a name and it was Sir, which seemed like an okay name. As fine as anything else, I guess.

The next few hours were a blur. I was mostly quiet and so was my family. We talked a little bit about the times we'd had together and everyone tried to be excited for me, but it was like how it always is when someone gets Taken. It is Sadhappy.

Man came into World after a while and he had the Taken Robe with him, which is a see-through cover that he puts over the top of you. Man said, "Okay, buddy. Let's get you ready to go." I don't know who Buddy is. Man never called me anything but Fiddle Ficus so I don't know who Buddy is or if I am Buddy. I don't know still if I am Buddy or Fiddle or Buddy Fiddle Ficus or Ficus Buddy Fiddle. Or Buddy Ficus. I know to me I am Fiddle, so I am going to just always be Fiddle to myself and if someone else wants to call me Buddy, I guess that's okay. One time a Human Person called Man "FRANK" and so maybe this is like that.

Man picked me up and put me on a moving cart and pushed me away from my family and past all my other friends. They all said good-bye and it was really sad. Nobody ever comes back to World after they leave. And I love World. I have everything I need here, and I love Man. What if Sir didn't treat me like Man?

I was feeling really not myself, and I don't remember much after leaving World. Too many feelings I have not felt before. Man put me into another World where there were no other trees, just a big World and me in it. I was under my Taken Robe and didn't see much. Man said, "Be good." And then he shut the door and it was Dark.

When it was Light again, another Human Person lifted me up and took me into another World, which is where I'm writing to you now. New World.

I can't see much of New World yet. I still have my Taken Robe on. Maybe I'll always have my Taken Robe on forever now. I don't know what the rules are of New World. I hope it's not a rule here, though, because I feel heavy and it's hard to keep my leaves Full.

I'm tired now from everything that happened. It's Dark now, I can tell. I am going to sleep now and hope that when I wake up it is Light. I hope that Light comes in New World, too.

October 16, 2015

Dear Journal,

Where to begin? Today was my first Light in New World. I didn't know what to expect, but this is so different from anything I could have expected.

As it turns out, where I spent Dark last night was not New World. When I woke up, I still had the Taken Robe on and was being picked up by Human People and moved. All of a sudden, there was a very brilliant bright Light. The brightest Light I had ever been in. It was like the World was all Light. Everywhere I looked, it was Light. Light walls, Light floors, and then real Light. The kind from Old World. The kind that makes me warm. The Human People put me down on the Light floors and jiggled me around a bunch. They'd step back and stare at me and then jiggle me some more, all the time saying, "Is it big enough?" which was so scary because I was thinking, *For what? Sir thought I was big enough. He thought I was the biggest. So I don't know who these Human People are, and I still haven't seen Sir.* This is what I'm thinking, you know? But I was worried, because what happens if these Human People think I'm too small? What happens then? Do I get Taken again? Some part of me thinks you can only get Taken once. There's only one chance. It's a Dark thought.

So I was just sitting in my New World, taking it in. Let me tell you about it.

It's all very Bright and Light from the Sunshine, which is very good, because like I said, I like Light. There is not a single other Tree in this New World except for me, which makes me feel very important but also it's a lot of pressure and I'm worried I'm going to get lonely. And also, what am I supposed to do? In Old World, I used to just talk to my family and my friends and have my Drinks and my Light. There was just a real sense of purpose, having all of us together in the same World. We just wanted to make Man happy and be ourselves in our way. I could just be Fiddle all day and that was okay.

Here in New World, it seems like since I'm the only one, I should be DOING SOMETHING, or maybe I'm not impressive enough to be the only one here. Why me? I am trying to remember that if I got Taken, it is because I am the right ficus for this New World.

There are Shiny things attached to the ceiling, and Human People call them "Lights." ??????????? I don't get this. They give off Light but it's not like the kind of Light I am used to. It's more like flat. It's hard to explain. It's not Sunshine, but everyone is pointing at them and calling them "Lights" so this is something I don't understand yet, but I will keep listening and let you know.

There are white boxes everywhere, and inside of the walls there are holes, but they aren't holes because they are long squares and very smooth, not like an On Accident. I don't know what they're for or why. Same with the boxes. Maybe they don't know why they're here either, like me. Everything is very smooth. The walls, the floor, the boxes, the square wall holes. It is like very perfect and very Shiny. It makes me feel a little embarrassed because I know that I am not exactly perfect in this same way. I am not all Light. I am not very smooth everywhere. I am hoping I am still very Shiny. At least I can be Shiny. Maybe not as Shiny as the LIGHTS, but still Shiny in my Fiddle way.

Here's the most craziest thing about New World. I sit in front of something the Human People are calling Window. Window is like a more clear Taken Robe. I can see straight through it and past it forever. So when I look out Window, there is an entire OTHER WORLD. And right in front of me is ANOTHER TREE!!!!!!!!!!!!!!!!!!!!!

I was so excited when I saw him, I was sure I was shaking. I screamed HELLO HELLO HELLO LINDEN TREE! OVER HERE! INSIDE THE LIGHT BOX! But Linden Tree didn't answer. It was like he didn't even see me. Or hear me. But how could he not see me if Window is clear? Maybe if I could work on Growing toward Window, then I could take my branches and leaves and hit Window and then Linden Tree would hear it or sense that I was there? I am going to think more about this.

I'm starting to wonder how many Worlds there are. Because just in not very

much time I have been in so many and they're all very different. What if the rules are that in Outside World, Linden Trees can't talk to anyone in New World?

All Light, people have been coming in and out and they're talking into their hands. They say things like, "WELL WHEN WILL THEY ARRIVE?!" "WE OPEN IN TWO DAYS, ANTHONY," "I DON'T HAVE FUCKING TIME FOR THIS. I NEED CARRARA MARBLE CUBES AND I NEED THEM TODAY. ACTUALLY I NEEDED THEM YESTERDAY. FUCKING YESTERDAY, CAMILLE." And "THIS IS ON YOU." And "THIS IS CÉLINE, FOR GOD'S SAKE." What is Céline?

Everyone seems very mean and not very nice, but maybe that is just the way of New World and I, too, will eventually become very mean, though as I mentioned it is not in my ficus nature to be mean.

It is almost Dark. I will write you again after the next Light.

October 17, 2015

Dear Journal,

Something I learned today is that in this World, they call Light Today. When they say "Today" they are saying in the time that it is Light. I'm going to say it now instead of Light because I'm trying to fit in here in New World and trying to forget about Old World even though it is hard and I am really missing a lot of things.

So, TODAY (see?) a lot of things happened. At the beginning of Today, all the Human People came into World and were very busy, running around all over the place talking into their hands like they always are. But get this: I realized today that they aren't talking into their hands. They're talking into PHONES. I know this because the one Human Person called Anthony yelled at one point, "I CAN'T FIND MY GODDAMN PHONE," and then another Human Person said, "It's on the Display Cube." So this was very important because I learned that the Human People are talking into their Phones, and the Light Boxes are called "DISPLAY CUBES." Phone seems very important in New World, because everyone always is talking on one or tapping on one and they just seem to control what is going on. I don't know if eventually I will get a Phone, too, or if it is just for Human People and Display Cubes and ficus trees don't get Phones.

Around the middle of Today, the MERCHANDISE arrived. "Merchandise" is a big word that means a lot of things. It is almost a word like "Tree" because it describes what I am but if you want to say specifically who I am, I am Ficus, and if you want to know more, my name is Fiddle. So like in the same way, there is Merchandise, and then there are different kinds. Here's what they are:

CLOTHES: Clothes are what Human People are wearing. They can be whatever color they want to be and they can be very long or very short or very wide. They can have Shiny things or not. They seem to be very important in New World. They all come in their own sort of Taken Robes. My Taken Robe is see-through, but theirs are Dark and they all say "C É L I N E" on them. So this "C É L I N E" word keeps coming up and I have some ideas about it but I will tell you later.

SHOES: Shoes are what Human People are putting on the bottom of them for moving around. Shoes seem important, but not as important as Clothes. They also come in a lot of different ways. Some of them are straight lines and some of them aren't. They come in whatever colors they want to and can have Shiny things or not, like how Clothes are. They ALSO arrived in Taken Robes that are Light and they ALSO say "C É L I N E" on them.

The most important kind of Merchandise, and maybe the most important things in all of New World, is BAGS. It is almost like how Light was in Old World, BAGS are in New World. It's weird, though, because they just come in regular "C É L I N E" Taken Robes like the other Merchandise, but all the Human People hold them very gently and pet them and say, "Oooohhh," and they say how beautiful they are and how amazing and they say they are "OBSESSED" with them. I don't totally understand this, because they seem like how the other Merchandises are, but almost, like, less important if you ask me, because Human People just hold them. They don't wear them like CLOTHES or SHOES. They just hold them on their arms or in their hands like PHONES. But they don't talk to them like PHONES, who (I think) can talk BACK to the Human People, though I have never heard them talk, so . . . But the BAGS don't talk or anything. They're just Shiny and very smooth and very Perfect.

So then, the Human People spent a very long time taking the Merchandise and putting it INTO the wall holes and setting things on the Display Cubes, and angling the Lights so they put their Shine onto the Merchandise, and it just seemed to be all about the Merchandise. And if I'm being really honest with you, it seemed like it was really all about the BAGS.

I guess I'm just feeling really Sad Today. I didn't know what to expect in New World, but the way things are turning out here, it doesn't seem like I really have much of a role. Or like, maybe In New World, Trees are less important than Merchandise, and specifically BAGS. Like, I am wondering if maybe this World is made for BAGS??

I don't mean to brag or anything, but in Old World, Trees were like BAGS. We were pretty important and there were a lot of us and Man treated us like how these Human People are treating Bags. And I'm just looking around and I realize that in New World, I'm more of like Wall Holes or Display Cubes or something. It seems like I am meant to be here just to watch the Merchandise get all the attention.

I'm trying to be happy for Merchandise and to understand my new role in this World, but I'm just feeling really Down.

To make things worse, I'm really Thirsty and I want a Drink, but nobody here even LOOKS at me, let alone comes by and pets my leaves and says, "How are we doing? You look thirsty." Like how Man used to. He always knew when

I was Thirsty. I'm realizing now that maybe these Human People don't know that I'm Thirsty and so how am I going to get a Drink?

I'm trying not to panic and to stay Full and Shiny, but it's getting harder to do.

October 18, 2015

Dear Journal,

Today was crazy.

I am feeling so many feelings right now, but let me start by telling you that I was right about almost everything I was saying about New World. It IS a world for Merchandise. Also, listen to this. I learned that the NAME of World is C É L I N E.

So, today was the OPENING of C É L I N E. What that means is that it's like how in Old World, Human People would come and look at all of us Trees and decide who to Take. It's like that for C É L I N E, too, but here, instead of it being for Trees, it's for Merchandise.

Here's what happens:

I see a Human Person outside of C É L I N E. I see them through Window. And they walk up to the doors, and two Dark Clothes Men open the doors of C É L I N E for them, and then they come inside. The Dark Clothes Men say, "Hello, welcome to C É L I N E." And the Human People usually say something nice to them back, like, "Hi, thank you," and then they look around C É L I N E.

They look up, and down, and at Lights and at MEEEEEE (!!!!!), and then they start to focus and start looking at Merchandise.

This is when things start to get crazy, or at least I think so.

So, in addition to the Dark Clothes Men, there are Associates. They are like how Man had Help at Old World. The Associates are like Help. They help

the Human People who enter C É L I N E to Take Merchandise. They tell them all about Shoes and Clothes and Bags. They say really nice things about all Merchandise. They say like, "Oh, isn't It so special?" "How incredible are Those?" "It's just an amazing Piece." (I have learned that you can say "Piece" when you want to talk about one kind of Clothes.) The Associates also are always running to the Back to bring out other kinds of Merchandise. I'm realizing that the Back is where I spent the one Dark before I started living in C É L I N E.

The Human People that come into C É L I N E are so happy to be in C É L I N E. It is like they are in a very special place and they are feeling very grateful to be there. Because they are very quiet and they are just saying, "Wow," and "So amazing" when they are looking at Merchandise. It almost sometimes seems like they are Sad they are so Happy. I only know how this feeling is because of how I sometimes felt in Old World when one of my brothers or sisters would get Taken. It was like two feelings at one time.

I was right about what I said about Bags. Bags are the most important in C É L I N E. When the Human People come in, a lot of them don't even look at Clothes or Shoes, they just go straight to Bags. They get really excited and they want to touch all of them and hold all of them and look in Mirror with all of them. They ask the Associates many many many questions about Bags.

And in the end, what seems to usually happen is that the Human People decide what Merchandise to Take. Sometimes it is all kinds. Sometimes it's Bags and Shoes and Clothes. Sometimes it's like three Bags. Sometimes it's one Shoes. But a LOT of Merchandise gets Taken. But here is something spooky: Once a Human Person says what they want to Take, the Associates go to the Back and bring out ANOTHER Bag or Shoes or Clothes Piece that is the SAME as what is on the Floor. (I can barely explain this. The Associates call C É L I N E "the Floor" like how they call the other World "the Back." I think they are all part of the same World, which is C É L I N E.)

So do you see what I am saying? The Merchandise on the Floor is not the

Only. There is another whole place in the Back where there is just even more of the exact same Merchandise. Like copies.

I'm not trying to say anything mean about Merchandise, it's just, I don't see why it is so special and so great if there is just the exact same thing in the Back. Like, with trees, there is just ME, FIDDLE. And I am very one of a kind, and that is like, a very cool thing. Or at least it was in Old World. We all were different and that is what made us very special, and that was sort of WHY we were picked for being Taken.

Here at **C É L I N E**, it's like, there aren't even that many kinds of Bags, and then there's like, an endless supply of identical Bags in the Back, so why do these Human People think these Bags are so important and special?? Why are they holding them so carefully, like if they jostle them the wrong way, they might ruin them? I want to shout, "HEY, HUMAN PERSON, DON'T YOU KNOW THE BAG YOU ARE HOLDING HAS BEEN HELD BY MANY PEOPLE BEFORE YOU AND THERE ARE TONS MORE JUST LIKE THEM IN THE BACK, AND LIKE, YOU ARE NOT THE FIRST HUMAN PERSON TO TAKE THAT BAG. IT'S BEEN TAKEN A LOT OF TIMES BEFORE NOW AND HUMAN PEOPLE WILL ALWAYS TAKE IT SO WHY ARE YOU BEING LIKE SO PRECIOUS AND CAREFUL WITH THIS PARTICULAR BAG LIKE IT IS SOMETHING UNIQUE?"

I would obviously never do that, because that's very mean to Bags, but it's just something I am thinking about privately.

So anyway, the Associates bring out the Back Merchandise in complicated Taken Robes and then the Associates and the Human People go to PAY.

PAY is a big deal in **C É L I N E**. In **C É L I N E**, it is on the same level of important as Bags are. Human People in **C É L I N E** are talking a lot about AFFORD and PAY. AFFORD means whether or not you can Take. AFFORD is GOOD. The Associates like AFFORD and want everyone to AFFORD. They're not mean to anyone if they can't AFFORD, but they seem to be able to tell if someone can AFFORD or not, and once they know someone can't AFFORD, they don't want to show them Merchandise as much anymore. I don't always know how they can tell, but they seem to usually know which Human People can AFFORD and which can't.

From what I can tell, the Shinier Human People who come in can AFFORD, and the less Shiny Human People cannot AFFORD, or at least cannot AFFORD to Take as much. It is not always true, though, because sometimes a Women (this is the kind of Human Person that comes into **C É L I N E**) will come in, and she isn't Shiny at all, but the Associates will get very excited about showing her the Merchandise and then all of a sudden she has Taken half of the Floor, and she leaves with all sorts of Merchandise.

And sometimes Women come in and they take a very long time and they like to touch everything and talk to all the Associates, and then they only Take like, one Clothes. This seems to make the Associates sad or mean. Other times, a Women will come in and spend not very long at all and talk to nobody and Take almost everything from the floor. Like she doesn't even care what it is that she is Taking, she just wants to Take as much as possible. I don't know why, because usually this Women doesn't even seem like she is happy when she Pays. It's the same as when she came into **C É L I N E**. Whereas sometimes a Women comes in and buys maybe one Shoes and she leaves **C É L I N E** and she is VERY Shiny and Full and happy. Those Women make ME happy because I feel proud to be in a World that makes Human People Shiny and Full.

OH! By the way, SIR came back this Today. Do you remember me telling you about Sir? It seems like a really long time ago, but he is the one who Takened me. He came back ESPECIALLY to check on me. He looked me up and down and even felt my leaves. He was looking at me very hard and from all the angles, and I was thinking, *HELLO I AM THIRSTY CAN YOU PLEASE JUST GIVE ME A FUCKING DRINK??????* ("Fucking" is a word you say when you are trying to make a point about something or trying to tell someone that you are not joking around and they need to really listen up.) Sir understood what I needed because he gave me a VERY big drink and so I'm feeling pretty good right now. Pretty happy about C É L I N E. I barely remember Old World anymore.

October 23, 2015

Dear Journal,

I'm beginning to really settle into my new life here at C É L I N E. I am still learning a lot every day. It's a complicated World.

I learned that you don't have to say Human People every time you want to talk about Human People. You can just say "People," because it is implied that they are Human. It's kind of obvious, but I didn't get it before.

For the most part, every Today is the same at C É L I N E. We OPEN, and then People come in, and then they Take the Merchandise and PAY for it if they can AFFORD it, and then they leave C É L I N E. It just goes on like this all Today until it's time for CLOSE. At CLOSE, other people, like the Associates, but in different Clothes, they come in and make everything Shiny again. Sometimes they even rub my leaves and make sure that I am Shiny, too. They come at the Tonight. Tonight is when it's Dark.

It's a peaceful World. I don't know what my role is in it, exactly. Maybe it is still to come, or maybe I am doing it right now. I know that I will not be Taken again. That is not my role. Maybe I am just supposed to sit here and be as Shiny and Full as I possibly can be. Like how Merchandise just sits around and looks Shiny and Perfect.

I will admit that I'm a little lonely.

One Tonight Associate is a Women People and she plays music out of her Phone while she makes C É L I N E Shiny, and she dances a little sometimes, and when she works on making me Shiny she will sometimes talk to me like

Man used to. She doesn't say a lot. She said to me one time, "Look at this, little buddy." I tried to explain to her carefully that I am fucking Fiddle, and not fucking Buddy, and I think on some level she understood because she didn't say it again. I think it was a good thing that I said the "fucking" word so she really understood.

Sometimes she sings and I am so happy when she does that. Man used to sing with his mouth hole closed.

I don't know if she has a name. The Associates all have names, but she is always alone so nobody ever calls her anything, so I don't know. I hope this isn't bad, but I am going to call her WOMAN. I am going to call her WOMAN because she is a WOMEN but she reminds me of MAN because she talks to me and checks on me. So she is WO-MAN. WOMAN.

So I am not as lonely when Woman comes.

October 25, 2015

Dear Journal,

A LIGHT went out today. It was shining directly on MEDIUM PHANTOM in RED on Display Cube Three, and then . . . it wasn't.

I don't know what to make of it. What does it mean? I didn't know it was sick.

In Old World, sometimes Trees would get sick, and then Man would take extra care of them and give them different Drinks or more Light and they would get better.

In C É L I N E, this Light just went Out like it was more than sick, like it was dead. And then do you know what happened? Nothing happened all today. The Associates didn't do a thing about it. They just let the dead Light stay there like nothing was wrong. The Manager, Anthony, who is like the most important Associate, he said, "They'll take care of it tonight."

And tonight, Woman climbed up into the ceiling and just replaced the dead Light with a new Light. Just like that. Didn't say anything, didn't try to help it. Just pulled it from the ceiling and put in another one. She got the new Light from the Back.

So now this has me thinking. Are there more Fiddles waiting in the Back? If I get sick, will Woman take care of me like how Man would have or will she just replace me like how the Bags and Shoes and Clothes get replaced all the time from the Back? I would like to think that Woman and I have established the kind of relationship where she would take care of me if I got sick, but who can say???? I know the Associates wouldn't care. It's like they don't even see me.

I haven't seen Sir since the last time I told you he gave me a Drink. Now Woman gives me my Drinks, so I guess I really misunderstood my relationship with Sir. Sir is not at ALL the new Man. Woman is Man.

November 1, 2015

Dear Journal,

Something very interesting happened today.

A Woman came into C É L I N E and she had a Bag with her in its Taken Robe, and she said to an Associate, "I want to return this." And the Associate said that it was not returnable, and she got very upset and was saying how as it turned out, she didn't like the Bag, and it wasn't right and she just would please like her MONEY back. So the Associate said, No, this is not possible you need a RECEIPT. And she said, I don't have my RECEIPT, and the Associate said, Well, I am so sorry it is unfortunately impossible and also I can tell from looking at this Bag that it has been used before and therefore we cannot accept it back. Then

the woman got very angry and she said, I would please like to speak to your Manager. And then the Associate got Anthony the Manager, and Anthony said, What can I help you with? And they went through the whole thing again.

Then Anthony said to her, Unfortunately, this Bag is not from C É L I N E. It is a FAKE. And then the woman got VERY VERY ANGRY, saying, This is not a FAKE. I spent good MONEY on this Bag. MONEY that I would like credited back to my card in full thank you very much. And Anthony started to get mean and he said, Unfortunately this is impossible. And the woman was very upset and she just turned around and walked away, leaving this Bag with Anthony.

So it was very dramatic. "DRAMATIC" is bad, and in fact, Anthony is using it often to talk about other Associates and when he says this about someone it is not good. Anthony is often saying DRAMATIC and CUNT in the same ways. So that is what happened this time. Anthony said to another Associate, "What an insane fucking cunt. GOD, that was DRAMATIC, wasn't it?" and the Associate said, "Like, yeah, and what do we do with this shitty fake Bag?" And Anthony says, "Throw it the fuck away." AND THEN THE ASSOCIATE DID! HE THREW IT THE FUCK AWAY.

I don't understand. First of all, where would this Woman get a fake bag from C É L I N E if it was not FROM C É L I N E? And also, what makes something from C É L I N E, anyway? I am not FROM C É L I N E. I am from World, and I got Takened here. So does that mean that I am Fake, too, since I came from a different world that is not C É L I N E? Does it mean that anything that is not from C É L I N E is bad and should be thrown away?

WOMAN is not from C É L I N E. In fact, THE ASSOCIATES aren't even from C É L I N E. You know what ELSE?? MERCHANDISE ISN'T EVEN FROM C É L I N E WHEN YOU REALLY THINK ABOUT IT! It all came the exact same way that I did. In Taken Robes. So what's the difference between the shitty fake Bag and the Bags that live inside of C É L I N E?

You know what I am starting to think?? That actually EVERYTHING is fake

in **C É L I N E**. That it is all fake. That the shitty fake bag is no better or worse than the Bag on Display Cube Three.

November 8, 2015

Dear Journal,

I don't know where to begin and I don't know how much time I have left here, so I'm going to write fast.

Late last Tonight, after CLOSED, all the Associates did not leave. They STAYED late into Tonight and TAKENED AWAY ALL OF MERCHANDISE. They put everything into Taken Robes and Takened it all to the Back!!!!!! EMPTY! EMPTY **C É L I N E** except for me and Lights and Display Cubes and Wall Holes. Just like in the beginning when I first came to **C É L I N E**!! So then I thought, *Hang on one minute, if we are going in reverse order right now, that means that Display Cubes should be next to be Taken out.* So I waited. And waited and waited. And nothing was happening. The Associates were just sort of wandering around the Floor and talking like it was normal.

I was like, did someone TAKE EVERYTHING?? Who could AFFORD EVERYTHING?? Sometimes people can AFFORD basically what feels like almost everything. But it's never everything, and always everything is replaced immediately from the back, so where is the replacement Merchandise???

But it never came. What came INSTEAD was ALL NEW ALL DIFFERENT MERCHANDISE. It was like the first day of **C É L I N E** all over again!!!

Everything looked the same . . . But it wasn't! It was different. There were different versions of MEDIUM RED PHANTOM. There were different versions of MEDIUM CLASSIC BAG in CALFSKIN. Different colors, different Shiny parts. But still the same. But different.

WHY?????????????

What was wrong with old Merchandise??? It still was getting Takened! Every day People came in and Takened Merchandise, so why are there all new but the same Merchandises?

It feels like for no reason, and I am just really scared right now. Am I next????? I came in with the old Merchandise, so am I old Merchandise now, too??

I am really stressed out, which is something Anthony always says that he is. I think this is what this is because I feel like loud noises and yelling and Thirsty.

Woman didn't even come this Tonight. (IS WOMAN OLD MERCHANDISE TOO????????)

I wish Woman would come because I need a Drink and I want her to touch my leaves and talk to me and sing.

November 10, 2015

Dear Journal,

Well, I am still here.

That is about all I can say. I am still here in **C É L I N E**.

After they Takened all the old Merchandise and replaced it with new Merchandise (the Associates are calling this a new DELIVERY. Whatever. I'm sick of their words. They call everything something it isn't. Clothes are always Clothes. They aren't PIECES. I think they just make words up to try to convince Women to Take things they maybe cannot even AFFORD), something very crazy happened.

Women started coming into **C É L I N E** like very often! Like all the time! Very busy! Always Women coming in about the new Delivery. And listen to this. They come in and they will go to Bags and they will hold up Bag that is the SAME almost as Bag in their hand and they say, "OH MY GOD I NEED THIS!"

and then Anthony or whoever will say, "Oh, isn't it amazing? Isn't it such a special Piece? Isn't it so unique? It's really gorgeous in the new color." And the Women will say, "I THINK I HAVE TO TAKE IT," and then they do the same thing in Shoes and in Clothes!!!! But the Women are already wearing all the things they are saying "Oh wow oh jeez oh how exciting how fresh how new" about.

??????????????????????????

I don't understand what is going on with these Women. It is like they don't remember that they came into C É L I N E and did all of this just not even that many Todays ago!!! And like they don't even notice that it is all the same Merchandise but hardly different!!!

And another thing!! Sometimes I look at these Women and they have on Clothes or Shoes or Bags that I do not recognize from old Merchandise. So what does that mean???? Does that mean that there are other Worlds to get Clothes and Bags and Shoes and the Women are going to THOSE WORLDS TOO and Taking from them also???

Do these Women just go from one World to another World, Taking Taking Taking every Today? What else do they do?? Is the only thing for them about Merchandise and replacing Merchandise? For how long?? How long will they do this?? Forever?

I can only assume that this has all been going on for quite some time now. I wonder how long C É L I N E has been a World. I wonder how many other Merchandise Worlds like C É L I N E there are. I wonder if there are Fiddles like me in all the other Merchandise Worlds who have their own Womans and their own feelings like I do.

It all makes me so tired. I just want to Drink and be in the Dark of Tonight. The Todays take so long to be over, and it takes so much energy just to be Full and Shiny. What's the point?

Sorry to be so fucking depressing.

November 15, 2015

Dear Journal,

They replaced Woman.

There is a new Women person, and she does not sing.

Not even with her mouth hole closed.

November 16, 2015

Dear Journal,

Something bad is happening.

I think that I am getting sick.

I didn't notice it at first; it was one of the Associates. She looked over at me and looked at me really hard for a second like she had never even seen me before in her life even though I have been here much fucking longer than she has. Anyway, she looked at me and she said, "Ew, Anthony, I think that plant is dying. It's got a brown leaf."

First of all, or like how Anthony sometimes says to an Associate, "FIRST OF ALL, BITCH . . ."

So, FIRST OF ALL, BITCH. I am not a PLANT, I am a TREE. And don't say "ew" to me, because I happen to think that YOU are very ew. Your fuzzies on your head are VERY brown and I have not said one word about it to you. AFTER THAT, sometimes Trees get a brown leaf. It is not that big of a deal and there are many reasons why a Tree can get a brown leaf. It just means I need some extra care and special Drinks. It happened to me once before in Old World, and Man had me feeling fine again within like not even that many Todays. Some of the Drinks didn't even taste that bad.

So then Anthony comes over and looks at me very Dramatic, very Cunty, and he says, "Yeah, that's not cute. I'll call George."

Who the fuck is George?

I will say that I am feeling very tired lately. I feel worn out, and I know I am not the Shiniest I have ever been. I know I am maybe not the Fullest I have ever been. Not that I have been losing leaves or anything. It's not like that. I just feel sad more than anything. I just am feeling like all I want to do is be in the Dark where I can't really see Merchandise, and the Associates are gone, and I can just pretend I'm anywhere. Anywhere that isn't C É L I N E. Away from all the Lights and all the People and the PAYING and the AFFORD and the SPECIAL PIECES.

I miss my family. I miss my friends. I miss Man. I miss Old World. I wish I never got Taken. I wish I never even heard of C É L I N E or Bags or Clothes or Shoes.

November 17, 2015

Dear Journal,

Sir is George. George is Sir.

From what I understand, Sir is going to take care of me now that I am sick. He's going to check in with me more often to make sure I don't get browner or lose leaves. He gave me special drinks like Man did that one time.

It was nice to be looked at for once by someone. Nobody's really looked at me since Woman got replaced.

Sir George looks at me really hard. He looks mad. He doesn't really touch me.

I'm still tired but maybe the Drinks will help.

November 18, 2015

Dear Journal,

I'm feeling a little better, I guess. I don't know. I feel really far away lately. Like I am not even in C É L I N E at all and am in some other World that I haven't ever even been to.

It's not like I can imagine it, but it's more like I can feel how it would be. I can feel how it wouldn't be. It wouldn't be like C É L I N E. There wouldn't be the Associates or Merchandise. It would be more like Old World, but not even quite like Old World, because in my imagined World, nobody could ever get Takened. I could just be Fiddle. I could just be Fiddle all the Todays without any worries or anything. I could just get my Light and get my Drinks and be me.

I've been looking out Window lately and looking at Linden Tree. We have never spoken. It's like it doesn't even know C É L I N E exists even though it is right outside of C É L I N E. I wonder what its World is like out there.

Sometimes when it is Dark in the Today, Drinks come down from somewhere I can't see. Sometimes they come down for a very long time and I think, *Wow, that seems really nice for Linden. Just to have drinks fall down on your leaves for such a long time and for the Light to come down straight on top of your leaves.*

I have only had the Light come through a Window. I wonder what it's like if it comes down right on you.

Maybe Linden doesn't know anything even about Women or Men or People or Merchandise. Maybe it only knows about itself and Light and Drinks. I wish that was my World.

November 24, 2015

Dear Journal,

Sir George came again today. He is not "pleased" with my progress. He doesn't think I'm getting better and I don't really, either. I lost a leaf. Well, I lost two leaves, but that is only because Anthony jostled me when he was trying to pick up the first leaf off the ground and then another one fell off. So that is more on Anthony and not on me. That is more of Anthony's fucking problem, as Anthony would say.

Sir George gave me more Drinks and repositioned me slightly for more Light, but when he moved me, I realized now I can see myself in Mirror.

I haven't ever seen myself before, and it took me a while to realize it was me. But then I remembered that I am the only Fiddle in C É L I N E, and so it was clearly me.

I was shocked. I don't look very Shiny or Full. I look a little lopsided. And I look sick.

But then I got mad. So what if I look sick. I AM SICK. Why can't I be sick??? Am I supposed to be beautiful all the time?? For who?? Why?? Is my whole purpose in C É L I N E just to look nice??? What's so nice about looking nice??? I've looked nice my whole life and what has it gotten me?? Stuck in a corner of C É L I N E, alone, with no friends, no family, no LIFE.

I'm supposed to look beautiful to help Merchandise get Taken. You know what?? Merchandise would get Taken whether or not I was here.

These Women—they don't care if I'm here or not. They just want to Take Merchandise and then replace Merchandise forever. For always. For their whole lives. No little Fiddle Ficus is going to stop the Always of it.

If I got sicker, and if I were to die, I know now. I would just be replaced.

I was never special. It was never about me, just like it isn't about any one of the Bags. We are all just here in C É L I N E. For now. Until we aren't anymore.

November 26, 2015

Dear Journal,

I want to thank you for being my only friend here at **C É L I N E**. You and Woman were my only friends in this World, and I am very fucking grateful for you both. I don't think I am going to be here for very much longer in this World, and I don't know where I am going.

I am going to die. Sir George said so today.

I don't feel sad. I feel ready to leave **C É L I N E**.

I am a little scared, I will admit that. I don't know what will happen. Will I go to the Back? Will I just join all the old Merchandise in some other World?

I don't know the answer, but I know wherever I am going, it will not be like **C É L I N E**, and that makes me feel quiet in a good way.

Maybe I will go to a World like Linden's where the Drinks and the Light come down on top of me from above.

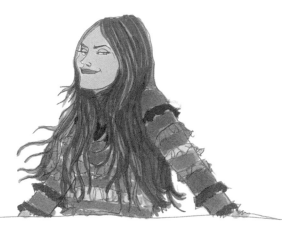
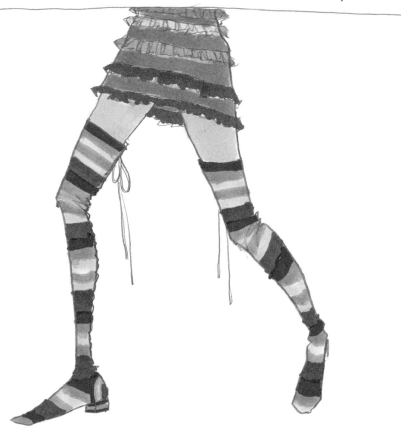

[insert inspiring message of hope]!!!

EVERYTHING HARPOONS FOR A RAISIN

I HAVE So MANY REGRETS

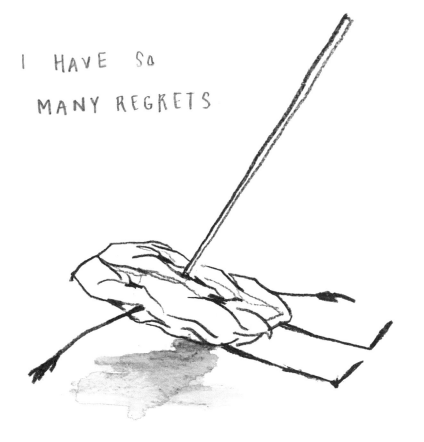

WHUT ARE YOU DOING?
YAH WHAT?

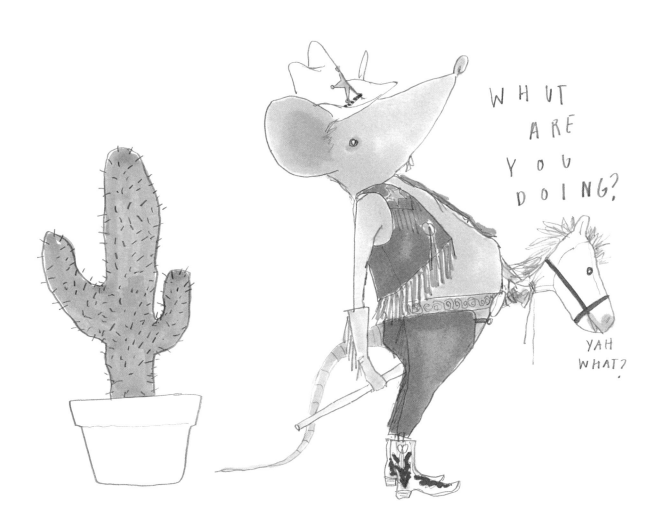

I AM DANCING
TO
DOLLY PARTON
IN A
TAKE OUT
CONTAINER
OF
TIKKA
MASALA

TIME TO MAKE
SOME LIFE-CHANGING
DECISIONS

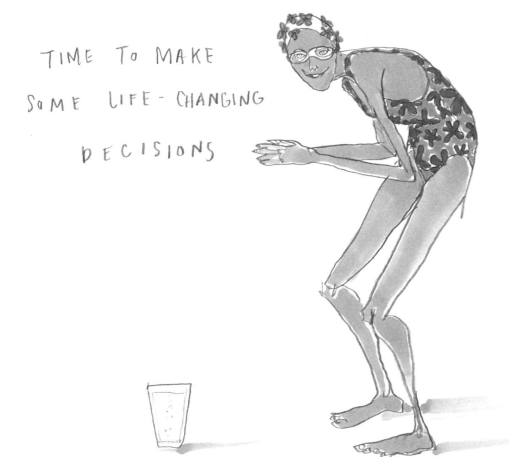

WHATEVER
FOREVER

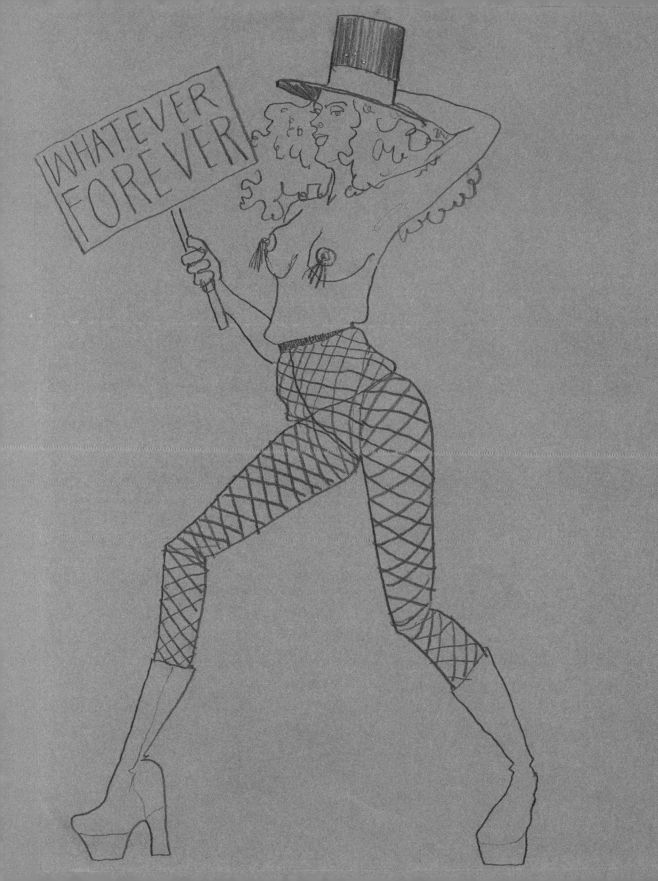

Thank you to my family, friends & gabe for all your love & support. Thank you Lauren & Alyssa for your endless patience & invaluable guidance. Thank you Seamless delivery men & indian food. I could not have done this without you. ♡♡

ABOUT THE AUTHOR

Julie Houts, otherwise known as @jooleeloren, is an illustrator and former womenswear designer at J.Crew. She was raised in Fort Wayne, Indiana, and St. Louis, Missouri, before studying at the School of the Art Institute of Chicago and Parsons School of Design in New York City. Her work has been featured in *Vogue, Nylon, Glamour, Man Repeller*, Stylebop, *The Huffington Post*, and *Refinery29*. Houts lives in Brooklyn.

JulieHouts.com

OK
BYE!!!!